A JOURNEY
TO THE CENTRE OF
THE EARTH

A JOURNEY
TO THE CENTRE OF
THE EARTH

JULES VERNE

Illustrated by John Howson

BLACKIE: LONDON AND GLASGOW

F

1880
/

ISBN 0 216 88506 X

Blackie & Son Limited
A Member of the Blackie Group
Furnival House
14/18 High Holborn
London WC1

Printed in Great Britain by
Robert MacLehose and Company Limited

CONTENTS

CONTENTS

BIOGRAPHICAL NOTE

Jules Verne was born in Nantes in 1828, studied law in Paris, and began his career as an author by writing libretti for two operettas, and a verse comedy in conjunction with Alexandre Dumas the younger. When he was 34, he published his first travel story, *Five Weeks in a Balloon*, and he followed this success with many others including *A Journey to the Centre of the Earth* in 1864, *Twenty Thousand Leagues Under the Sea* in 1869 and *Round the World in 80 Days* in 1872. He died at Amiens in 1905. The success of his stories as films shows that they are far from being overshadowed by our modern scientific world. Distinguished by a characteristic verve and humour, the work of this pioneer of science fiction is still as widely acclaimed as it was in his own lifetime.

*A JOURNEY
TO THE CENTRE OF
THE EARTH*

ONE

MY UNCLE LIDENBROCK

On the 24th of May, 1863, which was a Sunday, my uncle Professor Lidenbrock came hastily back to his little house, 19 Königstrasse. This is one of the oldest streets in the ancient quarter of Hamburg.

Our good Martha thought she must be behind with the dinner, for it was only just beginning to sizzle in the oven.

'Well,' I said to myself, 'if my uncle is hungry he will cry out, for he is the most impatient of men.'

'Mr. Lidenbrock here already!' cried the astounded Martha, looking in at the dining-room.

'Yes, Martha; but it's not time for dinner—it's not two o'clock yet. The half-hour has only just struck at St. Michael's.'

'Then why is Mr. Lidenbrock coming in?'

'He will probably tell us why.'

'Here he is! I'm off. Mr. Axel, you will get him to be sensible.'

And our good Martha went back to her culinary laboratory.

I stayed behind. But as to getting the most irascible of professors to be sensible, that was not a task suited to my rather undecided character. So I was meditating a prudent retreat to my little room in the attics, when the street door groaned on its hinges, heavy footsteps made the stairs creak, and the master of the house, passing through the dining-room, rushed hastily into his study.

But as he passed, he threw into a corner his stick with the nut-cracker head, on the table his broad hat, and at his nephew these emphatic words:

'Axel, follow me!'

Before I had time to move, the Professor shouted again in uncontrollable impatience:

'Well, you haven't come *yet*!'

I flew to the study of my formidable master.

Otto Lidenbrock was not, I freely confess, a *bad* man; but unless most unlikely changes take place, he will die in the skin of a very eccentric one!

He was a professor at the Johannæum, and gave a course of lectures on mineralogy, during which he constantly lost his temper. Not that he cared whether his pupils were punctual or attentive or successful—these details affected him but slightly. He was a 'subjective' professor, as the German philosophers would say, that is he lectured to himself rather than to others. He was a well of science, but the pulley creaked if one tried to draw anything out of it. A miser, in fact. Some German professors are like that.

My uncle, unfortunately, had a slight impediment in his speech, not so much in private as when he had to speak in public—which is a regrettable defect in an orator. Indeed, at the Johannæum, the professor would often stop short, struggling with an obstinate word which would not slip from his lips, one of those words which resist, swell up, and finally come out in the unscientific form of a swear-word!

In mineralogy there are many barbarous words, half Greek, half Latin, difficult to pronounce. Not a word would

I say against this science—far from it; but when one finds oneself in the presence of rhombohedric crystals, of molybdates of lead, tungstates of manganese, and titaniates of zircon, the most skilful tongue may be excused for slipping.

Now in the town the young fellows knew and took advantage of my uncle's pardonable infirmity; they listened for the dangerous passages, when he became furious, and then they laughed, which is not in good taste, even in Germany. So that of the large audience at the lectures, a certain number were undoubtedly present with the object of amusing themselves at the expense of the professor and his rages!

At any rate my uncle was most certainly a learned man. Though he sometimes broke his specimens by handling them too roughly, he added to the genius of the geologist the insight of the mineralogist. He made good use of his hammer, magnet, blow-pipe, bottle of nitric acid, etc. By the appearance, the fracture, hardness, fusibility, sound, smell, taste of any given mineral, he would unhesitatingly assign it to its place among the six hundred species known to science.

Thus the name of Lidenbrock was honourably mentioned in all scientific societies, and he had received visits from many distinguished foreigners, admirers of his *Treatise on Transcendant Crystallography*, a great folio volume, which, however, did not pay its own expenses.

This then was the person who called me with such impatience. Imagine a tall man, lean, in perfect health, and with a youthful complexion which took off a good ten of his fifty years. His great eyes were in constant motion behind big spectacles; his long thin nose was like a cutting blade— mischievous students asserted that it was magnetic, and attracted iron filings. But this was a calumny; it attracted only snuff, but that in great abundance.

When I add that my uncle's strides were mathematically three feet long, and that in walking he held his fists clenched (a sign of an impetuous temperament), you may perhaps understand him well enough not to be very anxious for his company.

He lived in his little house in the Königstrasse, half of wood, half of brick, opening on one of those winding canals which intersect the oldest quarter of Hamburg, mercifully spared by the fire of 1842.

My uncle was quite well off for a German professor. The house and its contents belonged to him—the latter including his god-daughter Gräuben, a native of the Vierlande near Hamburg, seventeen years old, our good Martha, and myself. In my double capacity of nephew and orphan, I became his laboratory assistant.

I must confess I delighted in geological work; I had the blood of a mineralogist in my veins, and I was never tired of the company of my precious pebbles.

Altogether, life went on happily in the little house in the Königstrasse, in spite of the proprietor's fits of impatience, for though his ways were rather violent, he loved me all the same. But he was incapable of waiting, and always in a hurry.

With such an eccentric, obedience was the only course. I therefore rushed to his study.

TWO

THE MYSTERIOUS PARCHMENT

This study was a regular museum. Specimens from every section of the mineral world were there, labelled with extreme exactitude.

How well I knew them! How often, instead of talking with boys of my own age, I had taken a pleasure in dusting these examples of graphite, anthracite, coal, lignite, peat! And those of bitumen, of resin, of organic salts which must be guarded from the slightest grain of dust! And the metals, from iron to gold, whose relative values were disregarded in view of their absolute equality as scientific specimens! And all those stones which would have sufficed to rebuild our house, with a delightful additional room, which would have suited me very well!

But as I entered the study, my mind was not on these marvels—my thoughts were entirely occupied with my uncle.

He was ensconced in his great Utrecht velvet arm-chair, holding a book at which he was gazing with the profoundest admiration.

'What a book! What a book!' he cried.

This exclamation reminded me that Professor Lidenbrock

was, in off hours, a book-lover; but the merit of a book in his eyes consisted in being unique, or illegible.

'Well,' he said, 'don't you see? I found this inestimable treasure this morning, hunting about at the book-shop of Hevelius the Jew.'

'Splendid!' I said, with forced enthusiasm.

After all, why this excitement about an old quarto volume, with back and sides made of coarse calf, yellowed by time, and with an old marker hanging from it?

But the professor continued to pour forth his admiration.

'Look!' he said, addressing and answering himself; 'isn't it beautiful? Yes, it is. And what a binding! Does it open easily? Yes, it stays open at any page you please. But does it close well? Yes, it closes without leaving the slightest gap. And the back has not the smallest crack, after seven centuries!'

So saying, my uncle opened and shut the old book several times. I could do no less than ask him what it was, though as a matter of fact I took no interest in the subject.

'This work,' replied my uncle with animation, 'is the *Heims-Kringla* of Snorro Turleson, the famous Icelandic writer of the twelfth century; it is the chronicle of the Norwegian princes who governed Iceland.'

'Really!' I cried, as heartily as I could. 'And no doubt this is a German translation?'

'A translation!' exclaimed my uncle. 'What should I be doing with a translation? This is the original work in the Icelandic language, which is both rich and simple, allowing of most varied grammatical combinations, and expressive of endless ideas!'

16

'Oh!' I said, beginning to be really interested; 'and is it good print?'

'*Print*, you idiot!' answered my uncle; 'it's a manuscript, a runic manuscript!'

'Runic?'

'Yes. Are you going to ask what that means?'

'Certainly not,' I answered, with an air of knowing all about it.

However, my uncle went on, informing me against my will of things which interested him far more than me.

'The runes,' he said, 'were letters of an alphabet formerly used in Iceland, and according to tradition, invented by Odin himself! Look, irreverent boy, these are the characters produced by the imagination of a god!'

My easiest answer might have been to prostrate myself, an answer which must give pleasure to gods as well as to kings, but I was saved the trouble by a curious incident—the sudden appearance of a soiled piece of parchment, which slipped out of the book and fell on the floor.

My uncle fell upon the fragment with an eagerness which will readily be conceived. An ancient document, shut, perhaps for centuries, between the pages of an old book, would of course be most valuable in his eyes.

'What is this?' he cried.

And at the same time he carefully unfolded on his table a piece of parchment five inches long and three broad, on which were extended in horizontal lines a number of unintelligible characters.

I append the exact facsimile. It is important to reproduce these curious letters, for they led Professor Lidenbrock and his nephew into the strangest adventure of the nineteenth century:

17

ᛉ.�505ᛙ   ᛙᚼᚻᛁᚻᛙᚿ   ᛌᛁᛁᚲᛁᛈᚿ
ᛒᛃᛁᚻᛃᛉᚷ   ᚾᛉᛁᛁᚷ   ᚠᛁᛁᛈᚻᛁᚾ
ᚷᛁᚼᛁᛁᛃᛉ   ᚻᛁᚼᚻᛁᛁᚼᚻ   ᚻᚾᚦᛈᚻᛉ
ᛁᛃᛁᛁᛒᛃᛁ   ᛉᚾᚻᚾᛁᛃ   ᚻᚻᚻᛁᚾᚻ
ᛁᛁᚾᚻᚻᚼ   .ᛉᛒᛈᛃ   ᛁᛈᚻᚻᛒᛙ
ᚷᛈᚾᚼᛁᛁ   ᛉᛁᚾᚼᛈᚿ   ᚠᚼᚻᚻᛈ
ᚾᛁᛙᛁᚼᛁ   ᚾᛙᚼᛁᛒᛉ   ᛁᛁᛈᛁᛁᛁ

The professor contemplated this series of characters for a
minute or two; then he said, pushing up his spectacles:

'It's runic; these letters are exactly the same as in the
manuscript by Snorro Turleson; but—what can it mean?'

I was not sorry to find that my uncle was mystified; his
fingers began to twitch terribly.

'And yet it must be ancient Icelandic!' he murmured; and
he ought to know, for he was a regular polyglot. He may not
have been able to speak all the two thousand languages and
four thousand dialects of the world, but he was acquainted
with a good proportion of them.

I foresaw a violent scene when two o'clock was struck by
the little clock on the mantelpiece.

Immediately Martha opened the study door, saying: 'The
soup is ready.'

'To the devil with the soup!' cried my uncle.

Martha fled; I ran after her, and by force of habit, found
myself at my usual place at the table.

I waited a few minutes. The professor failed, for the first
time in my experience, to grace the function of dinner. And
what a dinner! Parsley soup, an omelette of ham seasoned
with sorrel, veal with prune sauce, and for savoury, prawns
with sugar, the whole accompanied by excellent Moselle wine.

All this was lost to my uncle through an old scrap of
paper! Of course, as a devoted nephew, I considered it my

duty to eat for him as well as myself, and performed it conscientiously.

'I've never known such a thing,' said Martha, as she waited on me. 'Mr. Lidenbrock not at table!'

'It is really unheard of!'

'That means something's going to happen!' said the old servant, shaking her head.

In my opinion it meant nothing, but that there would be an awful scene when my uncle found that his dinner had been eaten.

I was just at the last prawn, when a stentorian voice dragged me from the pleasures of the table. With one bound I was in the study.

THREE

MY UNCLE IS PUZZLED

'It's certainly runic,' said the professor, frowning. 'But there's a secret, which I'll discover, or else——'

A violent gesture completed the idea.

'Sit down there,' he added, extending his fist toward the table, 'and write.'

In an instant I was ready.

'Now, I am going to dictate to you the letters of our alphabet which correspond with these Icelandic characters. We shall see what that gives us. But, by St. Michael! be careful not to make a mistake!'

The dictation began. I took great pains; the letters were called one after the other, and they formed the following incomprehensible series of words:

mm.rnlls	esreuel	seecJde
sgtssmf	unteief	niedrke
kt,samn	atrateS	Saodrrn
emtnaeI	nuaect	rrilSa
Atvaar	.nscrc	ieaabs
ccdrmi	eeutul	frantu
dt,iac	oseibo	KediiY

When I had finished, my uncle hastily seized the paper on

which I had just written, and examined it attentively for a long time.

'What can it mean?' he repeated mechanically.

On my honour, I couldn't tell. Besides, he was not asking me, and went on talking to himself:

'It's what they call a cryptogram, in which the sense is concealed by the intentional confusion of the letters; if they were rightly arranged, the meaning would be clear. To think that I may have here the exposition or at least an indication of some great discovery!'

On my part, I believed in nothing of the kind, but I discreetly kept my opinion to myself.

The professor then compared the book and the parchment. 'These are not by the same hand,' he said. 'The cryptogram is later than the book, as is absolutely proved by the double *m* which will certainly not occur in Turleson's book, for it was only added to the Icelandic alphabet in the fourteenth century. So there must be at least two hundred years between the dates of the book and the document.'

That, I admit, sounded convincing.

'I am therefore led to think,' continued my uncle, 'that one of the possessors of this book must have traced these mysterious characters. But who the devil was it? Won't he have written his name somewhere on the manuscript?'

My uncle pushed up his glasses, took a strong magnifying glass, and carefully examined the first pages of the book. At the back of the second, on which was the sub-title, he discovered a kind of blur, which looked like an ink-blot. But on further examination, half-obliterated letters could be made out. Finally, with the aid of the glass, he unhesitatingly read the following runic letters:

ᛧᛆᛒᛏ ᛌᛁᛘᛆᛊᛆᛊᛏᛜ

Arne Saknussemm!' he cried triumphantly. 'Now that's a name, and an Icelandic name, the name of a celebrated alchemist of the sixteenth century!'

I looked at my uncle with a certain admiration.

'Those alchemists,' he added, 'were the only scientists of their time. Why should there not be a surprising invention hidden in that cryptogram? There must be. There *is*.'

This supposition set fire to the professor's imagination.

'Perhaps,' I ventured to reply; 'but what interest could this learned man have in hiding his wonderful discovery?'

'Why did he? Why? How should I know? Didn't Galileo do so with regard to Saturn? Anyway, we shall see; for I will have the secret of this document, and I will take neither food nor sleep till I have guessed it.'

'Oh!' I thought.

'No more will you, Axel,' he added.

'Heavens!' I thought, 'it's just as well I had a double dinner!'

'Now first,' said my uncle, 'we must find the key to the cipher. That ought not to be difficult.'

He went on talking to himself.

'Nothing is simpler. There are in this document 132 letters, 79 consonants, and 53 vowels. Now that is about the proportion which obtains in southern languages, while the northern are far richer in consonants. So it is in a southern language. But what?'

'Just so—what?' I said to myself, but I was impressed by his analysis.

'This Saknussemm,' he continued, 'was a learned man, so

when not using his own vernacular, he would be sure to write in the common language of science in the sixteenth century, namely Latin. If I am wrong, I can try Spanish, French, Italian, Greek, and Hebrew. But Latin is the most probable.'

I jumped up. 'How could that stuff be Latin?'

'Yes, Latin, but in a confused form,' said my uncle.

'You will be clever if you manage to unravel it,' I thought.

'There is some key,' said my uncle, 'to the apparent confusion of these letters. But what is it? Axel, have you the key?'

To this I made no reply, for a good reason. My gaze was fixed on a charming portrait hanging on the wall, that of Gräuben. My uncle's ward was at Altona just then, staying with one of her relations, and her absence saddened me, for I may now confess that the pretty girl and the professor's nephew loved each other with all the patience and tranquillity of the German nature; we were promised to each other, unknown to my uncle, who was too much absorbed in geology to enter into such sentiments. Gräuben was a lovely young thing, fair, with blue eyes, rather serious-minded, but none the less loving; I on my part adored her, and her image translated me in an instant from the world of realities to that of dreams and memories.

I was contemplating the faithful companion of my work and my pleasures. She helped me every day in my care of my uncle's precious specimens; she labelled them along with me. Oh, Gräuben was a great mineralogist! She loved to get to the bottom of difficult problems. What delightful hours we had passed in studying together, and how often I had envied the lot of those insensible stones, caressed by her sweet hands!

Then, when recreation time came, we went out together

along the shady walks of the Alster, and visited the old tàrred windmill which gives such a picturesque aspect to the end of the lake; on the way we would talk, holding each other's hands. Thus we would arrive at the bank of the Elbe, and after saying good-bye to the swans swimming amongst the great white water-lilies, we would return by the steamer.

At this point in my day-dream, my uncle, striking the table violently with his fist, brought me back to reality.

'Look here,' he said, 'the first idea which would suggest itself in order to confuse the letters would be, I should think, to write the words vertically instead of horizontally.'

'That's a good idea,' thought I.

'Let's see how that works. Axel, write a sentence of any sort on this bit of paper; but instead of placing the letters one after the other, put them in vertical columns, so as to get five or six columns.'

I understood what was wanted, and immediately wrote in the required fashion.

I	*o*	*m*	*y*	*i*	*r*
l	*u*	*u*	*d*	*t*	*ä*
o	*v*	*c*	*e*	*t*	*u*
v	*e*	*h*	*a*	*l*	*b*
e	*r*	*,*	*r*	*e*	*e*
y	*y*	*m*	*l*	*G*	*n*

'Good!' said the professor, without reading it. 'Now arrange these combinations of letters in a horizontal line.'

I obeyed, and obtained the following:

Iomyir   luudtä   ovcetu   vehalb   er,ree   yymlGn

'Excellent!' cried my uncle, seizing the paper from my hands; 'that looks just like the old document: the vowels and consonants are grouped in the same fantastic way, and there are capital letters and commas in the middle of the words, as in Saknussemm's parchment!'

I couldn't help thinking that what he said was very ingenious.

'Now,' said my uncle, addressing me directly, 'to read the sentence which you have written, and of which I know nothing, all I need do is to take the first letter of each word, then the second letter, and so on.'

And my uncle, to my great surprise, and also to his own, read:

I love you very much, my dear little Gräuben.

'What?' said the professor.

Yes, without realizing it, the foolish lover had written down that compromising sentence!

'What! You are in love with Gräuben!' exclaimed my uncle in a severely magisterial manner.

'Yes—no——' I stammered.

'So you're in love with Gräuben!' he repeated mechanically. 'Well, now let us apply my method to the document in question!'

Returning to the absorbing subject, he had already forgotten my imprudence.

As he prepared to make the crucial attempt, the eyes of Professor Lidenbrock shot lightnings through his glasses; his fingers trembled as he took up the ancient parchment again; he was deeply moved. Finally he coughed loudly, and in a solemn voice called out to me successively the first letter of each word, and then the second letter of each, and so on, Thus he dictated the following series.

mmessunkaSenrA.icefdoK.segnittamurtn
ecertserrette, rotaivsadua, ednecsedsadne
lacartniiilu Jsiratrac Sarbmutabiledmek
meretarcsiluco Ysleffen Sn I

At the end, I must confess, I was excited. The letters as I put them down had conveyed nothing to my mind, but I expected the professor to produce some magnificent Latin sentence. But on the contrary the table was suddenly shaken by a violent blow from his fist. The ink spurted, and the pen flew out of my hand.

'It's wrong!' cried my uncle. 'There's no sense in it!'

Then, flying through the study like a bullet, descending the stairs like an avalanche, he flung himself into the König-strasse, and rushed along it as fast as he could go.

FOUR

I FIND THE KEY

'He's gone?' cried Martha, running up on hearing the violent bang of the street door, which shook the whole house.

'Yes,' I answered, 'gone right away!'

'Well, but what about his dinner?' asked the old servant.

'He won't take any.'

'But his supper?'

'He won't take any.'

'*What?*' cried Martha, clasping her hands.

'No, Martha, he will eat nothing, and no more will anybody else in the house. Uncle Lidenbrock is going to starve us till he has made out an old rigmarole that no human being can read!'

'Good gracious, then we must just die of hunger!'

I felt in my heart that, with a character as determined as my uncle's, it would really come to that.

The old servant, seriously alarmed, retired to her kitchen with groans.

When I was alone, I set to work to arrange a collection of geodes, those round hollow stones lined with crystals, which had recently been sent to my uncle by a French mineralogist. But while I examined and labelled these, and disposed them in their glass case, my mind was still preoccupied with the old document, and I had a presentiment of a coming catastrophe.

In an hour's time, my geodes being arranged, I seated myself in the big arm-chair, with my arms hanging and my head back, and watched the process which by slow degree was transforming the nymph on the bowl of my pipe into a negress. Meanwhile I almost unconsciously picked up the paper on which I had transcribed the letters dictated by my uncle. I could make no sense of it. At one moment I picked out the English words *ice* and *sir*, at another the Latin *rota*, *mutabile*, *ira*, *nec*, and *atra*, and then again the French *mère* and *arc*—but why all these languages, and what could the rest of the letters signify?

The difficulty seemed insoluble; my brain grew heated and the letters danced before my eyes. I felt stifled and in need of air. Mechanically, I began to fan myself with the paper, so that the back and front were alternately brought to view. What was my surprise, when at one of these rapid movements, at the instant when the back was just turning towards me, I seemed to be able to read Latin words, in particular *craterem* and *terrestre*.

Suddenly a light flashed on my mind; these indications gave me the key to the cipher. The reasonings of the professor were absolutely correct; he was right in the arrangement of the letters, right as to the language of the document. By one slight addition it would be possible to read the Latin sentence from beginning to end, and chance had presented me with that!

Of course I was full of excitement. My eyes would not serve me at first. I had spread open the paper on the table; I forced myself to walk twice round the room, then returned to the arm-chair, plunged into its depths, and gave the word of command, 'Read.'

Taking a deep breath, I leaned on the table, and placing my finger on each letter, without pause or hesitation I read the whole aloud.

But what terror and stupefaction it produced! I was thunderstruck. What! A man had had the audacity to penetrate——!

'Oh no!' I cried, leaping up; 'no, no, my uncle shall not hear of it! The next thing would be, if he knew of such a journey, that he would want to do the same! Nothing would prevent him—he would go in spite of all. And he would take me with him, and we should never come back. Never! Never!' I was in an indescribable state of super-excitement.

'No, it shall not be,' said I energetically, 'and since it is in my power to prevent such an idea from entering into the head of my tyrant, I will take steps to do so. If he keeps turning this paper about, he may discover the key. I'll destroy it.'

There was a little fire still burning. I picked up both my piece of paper, and Saknussemm's parchment; with feverish haste I was about to consign both to the flames and annihilate the dangerous secret, when the study door opened, and my uncle appeared.

I had only just time to replace the wretched thing on the table.

FIVE

MY UNCLE READS THE PARCHMENT

Professor Lidenbrock appeared deeply absorbed. His dominant idea gave him not a moment's respite; he had evidently analysed the matter and set to work all the forces of his imagination during his walk, and had returned to apply some new combination.

Down he sat in his arm-chair, and, pen in hand, began to work out what seemed like algebraical problems.

I followed with my eyes his quivering hand, without losing one of its movements. What unexpected result might follow? I trembled, foolishly, for as the true explanation had been found, any other was obviously doomed to disappointment.

For three long hours my uncle laboured without a word, without raising his head, crossing out and beginning again hundreds of times.

I knew very well that if he should succeed in arranging the letters in the proper order, the paragraph would be legible. But I also knew that the number of possible combinations of twenty letters only is 2,000,000,000, and that when it comes to the 132 letters which composed this document, the number of possible combinations is a number requiring 133 figures to represent it! Consequently there was no fear of my uncle finding the right one by exhausting all the others.

Well, night came on; the sounds in the street gradually ceased, my uncle, bent over his task, saw nothing else, not even Martha half opening the door; he heard nothing, not even the voice of the good old servant saying:

'Will you have your supper, sir?'

So Martha went away unregarded, and as for me, I fell asleep on the sofa, while my uncle continued to calculate and to cancel.

When I awoke in the morning, the indefatigable delver was still at work, but his red eyes, his pallor, his hair tumbled by his feverish fingers betrayed the severity of his terrible struggle with the impossible.

Indeed I was sorry for him. In spite of all, pity was gaining on me. The poor man was so possessed by his idea that he forgot to be angry; all his forces were concentrated on one sole end, and as they had no outlet, it was to be feared that there would be some injurious result.

By a word I could loosen the pressure of that steel vice which was squeezing his poor brain—by one word! And I said nothing.

I said to myself: 'No, no, I will not speak—I know him, he would want to go; nothing would stop him. He has a volcanic imagination, and would risk his life to do what other geologists have not done. I will keep the secret—let him guess it if he can, but I will not be responsible for sending him to his death.'

So I crossed my arms resolutely and waited. But I had reckoned without my host.

When Martha tried to go out to the market, she found the door fastened, and the great key was not in the lock. Who had taken it? My uncle must have done so when he came in the night before.

Was that intentional or not? Were we to be starved, Martha and myself, who were really in no way concerned in his problem? That would be going rather far—and yet I had an alarming recollection of another occasion, when my uncle was hard at work on his great mineralogical classification, and fasted for forty-eight hours, and all his household were obliged to do the same! I had a vivid memory of the internal pains which I, as a boy with an excellent appetite, had suffered in consequence. Besides, I longed to be able to leave the house and make my way to Altona to visit Gräuben.

I held out till two o'clock. By that time the arguments for

disclosure were taking on a very different aspect. I said to myself that I was exaggerating the importance of the document, that my uncle would not believe in it, that he would realize it to be a mere mystification, that if the worst came to the worst, he could be forcibly prevented from going; finally that if he were to find out the key of the cipher for himself, I should have fasted in vain.

All these arguments, which yesterday I had rejected with contempt, now appeared to me unanswerable, and I decided on immediate confession.

I was considering how to lead up to the subject, when my uncle stood up, put on his hat, and prepared to go out.

What! let him leave the house, and lock us in again! Never!

'Uncle!' I said. He did not seem to hear. 'Uncle Lidenbrock!' I repeated louder.

'Well?' said he like a man just awake.

'About the key?'

'What key? The key of the front door?'

'No, the key of that document!'

The professor looked at me over his spectacles; no doubt he saw something strange in my expression, for he seized me by the arm and looked a question which could not have been clearer, though it was not expressed in words.

I nodded my head.

He shook his pityingly, as if he feared for my reason.

I nodded more emphatically.

His eyes shone—I feared to speak, lest he should stifle me in his transports of joy. But he became so pressing that I was obliged to reply.

'Well,' I said, 'as to the key, by chance I——'

'What do you mean?' he cried, with indescribable emotion.

'Look,' I said, handing him the paper on which I had written; 'read it.'

'But it makes nonsense!' he replied, crumpling the page.

'Yes, if you start from the beginning, but, reading *backwards*——'

Before I had finished my sentence the professor gave vent to a cry, or rather a roar! It was a revelation, and he was transfigured.

Seizing the paper, with dim eyes and broken voice, he read the whole document, working from below upwards. It was expressed in these words:

> *In Sneffels Yoculis craterem kem delibat*
> *umbra Scartaris Julii intra calendas descende,*
> *audas viator, et terrestre centrum attinges.*
> *Kod feci. Arne Saknussemm.*

Which barbaric Latin may be thus translated:

Descend the crater of Snaefells Jokul, on which the shadow of Scartaris falls before the kalends of July, bold explorer, and you will reach the centre of the earth. I have done it. Arne Saknussemm.

On reading this, my uncle leapt as if he had unexpectedly received an electric shock. He became sublime in his courage, joy, and faith. He tramped up and down, held his head in both hands, moved the chairs about, piled up the books, played the most dangerous tricks with the precious geodes. At last his nerves were to some extent tranquillized, and he sank exhausted into his chair.

'What time is it?' he asked, after a few minutes silence.

'Three o'clock,' I answered.

'Is it? I'm hungry now. We'll go to dinner. And then ——'

'Yes?'

'Then you'll pack my box.'

'Pack your box!' I exclaimed.

'And your own,' said the pitiless professor, entering the dining-room.

SIX

ARGUMENTS

At these words, a shiver ran through my whole body. However, I preserved a calm exterior. I knew that scientific arguments alone could influence Professor Lidenbrock—well, I could produce good ones against the possibility of such a journey. To go to the centre of the earth! What an insane idea! But I reserved my attack, and went on to the dining-room.

I will not repeat the imprecations of my uncle on finding nothing ready! Explanations followed—Martha received her liberty, flew to the market, and managed so well that an hour later our hunger was appeased.

After dinner, my uncle signed to me to follow him to the study. There he said to me in quite a gentle tone:

'Axel, you are a very ingenious boy, and have rendered me a great service. I will never forget it, my boy, and you shall have your share in the glory we shall reap.'

'Good!' I thought, 'he's in an amiable mood; it's a favourable time to discuss that said glory.'

'Above all,' resumed my uncle, 'I insist on absolute secrecy, you understand. There are many rivals of mine who would be keen to undertake such a journey, but they shall only hear of it when it is accomplished.'

'Do you think,' I asked, 'that there would really be many who would risk it?'

'Certainly! Who would hesitate, with such fame to be acquired? If this document were known, a whole army of geologists would hasten to follow the traces of Arne Saknussemm!'

'I am not sure of that, Uncle, for I doubt whether the document is authentic.'

'What! When it was found in that book!'

'I agree that Saknussemm wrote the words, but it does not follow that he really performed the journey—may not the whole thing be a mystification?'

This was a risky word, but my uncle only said amiably:

'We shall see. Bring forward all your objections, my boy. I consider you no longer as my nephew, but as my colleague. Go on.'

'Well, first I should like to know the meaning of Jokul, Sneffels, and Scartaris; I have never heard of any of them.'

'Certainly. I have fortunately received lately from a friend a map which will help us. Take the third atlas in the second bay of the library, letter Z, fourth shelf.'

Obeying these very precise instructions, I at once found the required atlas. My uncle opened it and said:

'Here is one of the best maps of Iceland, Handerson's, and I think it will solve your difficulties.'

I bent over the atlas.

'You see all these volcanoes,' said my uncle; 'notice that they are all called *Jokul*. The word means *glacier*, and in those high latitudes the eruptions do really take place in the midst of ice.'

'Well,' I answered, 'but what is *Sneffels*?'

'*Snaefells*, as it should be written,' replied my uncle, 'is this mountain on a peninsula to the north-west of Reykjawik, the capital of Iceland. It is about 5000 feet high, and is one of the most remarkable mountains in the island—and indeed will be the most celebrated on earth, if its crater leads to the centre of the globe.'

'But it's impossible!' I cried, shrugging my shoulders in disgust.

'And why impossible, may I ask?' said the professor severely.

'Because the crater must be full of burning lava, and so——'

'But if it's an *extinct* volcano? The number of volcanoes now active is only about 300; but there are a great many more which are extinct. Now Snaefells belongs to these latter, and has had only one eruption in recorded times, namely that of 1229; since then it has been absolutely passive.'

I could but turn to my third difficulty. 'What does Scartaris mean?' I asked. 'And how do the kalends of July come in?'

My uncle considered for a few minutes, affording me a swiftly vanishing ray of hope, then he answered:

'This proves the ingenious care with which Saknussemm has provided us with exact instructions. Snaefells has several craters, so to indicate the one which leads to the centre of the earth, the wise Icelander has made use of the observation that at the approach of the kalends of July, that is, at about the end of June, the shadow of Scartaris, one of the peaks of the mountain, is thrown on the crater in question (at midday, no doubt). Could anything be more exact and helpful?'

He had an answer to everything. However, I passed on to more serious difficulties.

'Well,' I said, 'perhaps the old alchemist did go to Snae-fells, and did see the shadow of Scartaris on the crater; and perhaps he heard wild legends of the crater leading to the centre of the earth; but as to his having gone down there and come back alive, no, a hundred times no!'

'And why not?' asked my uncle, with an air of gentle mockery.

'Because all the theories of science prove that such a thing is impossible!'

'Oh, the theories prove it, do they? Poor old theories, what a nuisance they are!'

I saw he was jeering, but I went on.

'Yes, it is well known that the temperature rises about 1° C. for every seventy feet downwards, so that if this continues to hold good, the radius of the earth being more than four thousand miles, the temperature at the centre would be about two million degrees. Everything there must be in the state of incandescent gas, for gold, platinum, and the hardest rocks cannot resist such a temperature. How then could it be possible to go there?'

'So it's the temperature that worries you, Axel, and you are afraid of being melted?'

'I leave you to decide the question,' I answered crossly.

'This is what I decide,' said the professor, with a superior air. 'Neither you nor anyone knows exactly the condition of the interior of the earth, as we have only penetrated to about a twelve-thousandth part of its radius; but we do know that scientific theories are incessantly altered and improved. Besides, it is impossible that the centre of the earth should be gaseous, for the density of the whole earth is more than twice as great as that of the part we know. Then, too, it is an undoubted fact that the number of active volcanoes tends to diminish, showing that the internal heat of the earth is decreasing.'

'But surely the crust is the part which is cooling, while the original heat remains in the interior?'

'I believe that is a mistake,' replied my uncle. 'It is the *surface* of the earth which was heated, by combustion. It is composed in great part of metals, such as sodium and potassium, which catch fire by mere contact with air and water; this took place whenever rain fell, and as the water penetrated the cracks in the earth's crust, further combustion took place, causing explosions and eruptions.'

'That's an ingenious hypothesis!' I exclaimed.

'It was suggested by Sir Humphry Davy, who once paid me a visit,' said my uncle. 'He demonstrated the idea by making a little sphere, principally of the metals I have mentioned, and allowing a fine dew to form upon its surface at one point. Immediately that part swelled up and formed a little mountain; an eruption took place, and the whole ball became so hot that it could not be held in the hand.'

I began to be shaken by the professor's arguments, which he brought forward with his usual vigour and enthusiasm.

'Well, we shall see for ourselves,' he finished triumphantly; 'but silence, you understand, absolute silence about everything; let no one reach the centre of the earth before us!'

SEVEN

PREPARATIONS

So ended this memorable interview, leaving me in a feverish state of mind. I left my uncle's study as in a dream, and as there was not enough air in the streets of Hamburg, I made my way to the bank of the Elbe.

Was I convinced by what I had heard? Yes, I remembered that I had been convinced, though just now my enthusiasm was cooling; I should have liked to start at once, so as to give no further time for reflection. Yes, I should have had the courage to pack and strap up my bag that minute.

But an hour later my excitement had cooled, and I rose from the depths of the earth to the surface.

'It's absurd!' I cried. 'There's no sense in it. What a ridiculous plan! There's some mistake—I must have had a bad dream.'

Meanwhile I was following the bank of the river, had left the town and was on the road to Altona, led by a presentiment, which was soon justified, for sure enough, there was my little Gräuben walking briskly and vigorously towards Hamburg.

'Gräuben!' I cried when I saw her.

The girl stopped, apparently a little upset at hearing her name called on the high road.

A dozen strides, and I was at her side.

'Axel!' she exclaimed in surprise. 'Oh! you have come to meet me. I see.'

But she evidently noticed something peculiar in my expression—something restless and anxious.

'What is the matter?' she asked, holding out her hand.

A few sentences from me sufficed to put her in possession of the facts. For some minutes she was silent, and whether or not her heart was beating like mine, the hand which I held did not tremble. We walked perhaps a hundred paces together before she said:

'Axel!'

'Yes, dear Gräuben.'

'That will be a grand journey.'

I started violently at these words.

'Yes, Axel, and worthy of the nephew of a scientist. It is a good thing for a man to distinguish himself by some great enterprise.'

'What, Gräuben, you don't dissuade me from an expedition like that?'

'No, dear Axel, and I would willingly come with you and your uncle, if a girl would not be a hindrance to you.'

Oh, how incomprehensible is a girl's heart! When they are not the most timid of beings, they are the bravest! This girl was encouraging me to take part in the mad expedition, and would not have been afraid to venture herself. She was urging me to it—and yet she certainly loved me.

I was disconcerted, and, I must admit, ashamed.

'Well, Gräuben,' I replied, 'we shall see if you say the same tomorrow.'

'Tomorrow, dear Axel, I shall speak exactly as I have done today.'

We went on our way. I thought to myself: 'After all, the

kalends of July are a long way off, and many things may happen in between to cure my uncle of his mania for an underground expedition.'

It was night when we arrived at the Königstrasse, and I expected to find my uncle in bed, and Martha just completing the tidying of the dining-room.

But I had underestimated my uncle's impatience; I found him hurrying about and issuing orders to a number of men discharging goods at our entrance; the old servant did not know where to turn.

'Come along, Axel,' he cried as soon as he saw me, 'hurry up! Your box isn't packed, nor my papers arranged, and I can't find the key of my bag, and my gaiters haven't been sent!'

I was thunderstruck. I could hardly articulate: 'Are we going then?'

'Of course, you young fool, and you go out for walks instead of being at hand!'

'We're going?' I repeated feebly.

'Yes, first thing the day after tomorrow.'

There was no longer any doubt about it; my uncle had spent his afternoon in procuring some of the things required for the expedition, and the gravel-path was heaped with knotted-rope ladders, torches, flasks, pick-axes, iron-shod poles, and so on, a sufficient load for ten men!

I passed an awful night. Next morning I was called early. I had made up my mind not to open my door. But how could I resist the gentle voice which said: 'Dear Axel!'

I came out, hoping that my pallor and red eyes, the effect of a sleepless night, would change Gräuben's ideas.

'Ah, dear Axel,' she said, 'I see you are better and that the night has calmed you.'

'*Calmed* me!' I said to myself. I flew to the looking-glass. Well, I *didn't* look as ill as I expected. I could hardly believe it.

'Axel,' said Gräuben, 'I have had a long talk with my guardian. He's a great man, and full of courage and you have the same blood in your veins. He has told me of his projects and his hopes, and why and how he expects to attain his end. He will, I am sure. Oh, Axel dear, it's splendid to devote oneself to science! What glory is in store for Mr. Lidenbrock—and his companion! When you come back, Axel, you will be a man, his equal, free to speak and act, free to——'

She stopped short, and blushed. Her words revived my courage. However, I was still doubtful. I drew her towards the professor's study.

'Uncle,' I said, 'are we really going?'

'Of course we are. Why?'

'Well, I only wanted to know why we're hurrying. It's only the twenty-sixth of May, and we have till the end of June——'

'But are you so stupid as not to know that it takes time getting to Iceland? If you hadn't gone off like a fool, I should have taken you with me to the office of Liffender & Co., who run the ships between Copenhagen and Reykjawik; there's only the one service.'

'Well, Uncle?'

'Well, if we were to wait till 22nd June, we should be too late for the shadow of Scartaris on the crater of Snaefells; so we must get to Copenhagen as quickly as we can, and see what we can find. Go and pack your things!'

There was nothing to be said. I went back to my room, accompanied by Gräuben. She it was who undertook the packing, in a small portmanteau, of the clothes necessary for my journey. She was no more agitated than if I had been taking a trip to Lübeck or Heligoland; her little hands performed their functions without undue haste, and meanwhile she talked calmly and hopefully. She enchanted me, and yet made me very angry. Sometimes I lost my temper, but she took no notice of it and continued her work quietly.

At last the last strap was buckled, and I went downstairs.

All day physical instruments, fire-arms, electrical apparatus had been arriving. Poor Martha was quite losing her head.

'Is the master out of his mind?' she asked me.

I nodded.

'And he's taking you with him?'

I repeated the gesture.

'Where are you going?'

I pointed towards the centre of the earth.

'Into the cellar?'

'Deeper down,' I said, forced at last to speak.

The night came before I expected it.

'Tomorrow morning,' said my uncle, 'we set off at six sharp.'

At ten I sank like a log upon my bed. But during the night my fears returned. I dreamed of abysses. I was almost delirious. I felt myself dragged by the strong hand of the professor into hollows and quicksands. I was falling from the top of infinite precipices with the acceleration of bodies in space. My life became one interminable fall.

I woke at five, worn out with fatigue and emotion. I went down to the dining-room and found my uncle at table, eating voraciously. The sight disgusted me; but Gräuben was there. I was silent, and could not eat.

At half-past five, wheels were heard outside. A big carriage was there to take us to the station at Altona. It was soon filled with my uncle's belongings.

'Where's your luggage?' he asked me.

'It's ready,' I faltered.

'Be quick and bring it down then, or you'll make us miss the train!'

It seemed impossible to resist my fate. I went up to my room again, and letting my portmanteau slide down the stairs, I ran after it.

My uncle was solemnly confiding the 'reins' of the house into Gräuben's hands. The pretty dear was calm as ever. She embraced her guardian, but she could not restrain a tear as she touched my cheek with her sweet lips.

'Gräuben!' I cried.

'Go, Axel dear,' she said; 'you leave your betrothed, but when you come back you shall find your wife.'

I pressed her in my arms, and then took my seat in the carriage. Martha and she, from the threshold, waved a last good-bye, as the two horses set off at a gallop for Altona.

EIGHT

THE START

Altona, which is practically a suburb of Hamburg, is the railway terminus for the Kiel line which would take us to the shores of the Belts. In less than twenty minutes we were in the territory of Holstein.

At half past six we were at the station; my uncle's numerous and bulky articles of luggage were taken down, carried in, weighed, labelled, and placed in the luggage-van, and at seven we were seated opposite each other in one of the compartments. The whistle sounded, the train was in motion. We had started.

Was I resigned? Not yet. All the same, the fresh morning air, the novelty of the scenery through which the train rapidly carried us, distracted my thoughts.

As to my uncle's thoughts, they evidently went ahead of the train, which was far too slow for his impatience. We were alone in the carriage, but neither spoke. My uncle kept examining his pockets and his travelling-bag with minute care. I saw that he seemed to have thought of every possible requirement for the execution of his projects.

Amongst other things, a carefully-folded piece of paper, with the Danish arms, bore the signature of Mr. Christiansen, the Danish consul at Hamburg and a friend of the professor.

47

This was to enable us to obtain at Copenhagen introductions to the governor of Iceland.

I also perceived the famous document, carefully bestowed in the innermost pocket of his note-case. I cursed it heartily, and then gazed at the landscape again—a vast succession of uninteresting, monotonous, and fertile plains, favourable to those straight lines which rejoice the hearts of railway companies.

But I had not much time to tire of the monotony, for in three hours from the start the train stopped at Kiel, on the very edge of the sea.

As our luggage was registered for Copenhagen, we had no trouble with it. All the same, my uncle anxiously watched the conveyance of it to the steamer. There it vanished into the hold.

My uncle in his haste had allowed so much time that we had the whole day to spare—our steamer, the *Ellenora*, was only to sail at nightfall. So we passed a feverish nine hours, during which the irascible traveller poured forth imprecations on the management of railways and steamers, and on the Governments which tolerated such abuses. I was expected to support him when he interviewed the captain of the *Ellenora*, urging him to get up steam at once—but the captain appeared to think he knew his own business best.

At Kiel, as elsewhere, a day does somehow pass. By dint of wandering along the shores of the bay on which the little town stands, and through the woods which make it look like a nest amid twigs, admiring the villas, each provided with a little bathing-shed, trudging and complaining, we reached ten o'clock at night.

Columns of smoke were now rising from the funnel of the *Ellenora*; the deck was shaking with the throbbing of the boiler; we were on board and had taken possession of two berths in the only cabin.

At a quarter past ten the ropes were cast off, and the steamer made her rapid way across the dark waters of the Great Belt.

The night was dark; there was a favourable wind and a high sea; some lights along the coast shone through the night, and some time later a lighthouse brightly illuminated the tossing waves; that is all I remember of this first crossing.

At seven in the morning we disembarked at Korsör, a little town on the west coast of Zealand. There we boarded another train, which carried us in three hours to Copenhagen. My uncle had not slept all night. In his impatience, he seemed to be pushing the train forward with his feet.

At last he caught sight of a sheet of water. 'The Sound!' he cried.

There was a great building on our left which one of our travelling-companions declared to be a lunatic asylum.

'Good,' I thought, 'it would do very well for my uncle!'

At ten o'clock we alighted at Copenhagen, and we and our luggage were conveyed to the Phœnix Hotel in the Bred-Gade. Then my uncle, after a hasty toilet, carried me off. The hotel porter spoke both German and English; but the polyglot professor made his inquiries in good Danish, and obtained instructions as to the situation of the Museum of Northern Antiquities.

The curator, Mr. Thomsen, a very learned man, was a friend of the consul at Hamburg, and received Professor Lidenbrock, and indeed his nephew too, most kindly and cordially. I need scarcely say that we kept our secret, and were simply tourists interested in the wonders of Iceland.

Mr. Thomsen put himself at our disposal, and took us to

the quays to find a vessel leaving for that island. I myself hoped against hope that there would be none; but to my disappointment, a little Danish schooner, the *Valkyrie*, was to sail for Reykjawik on the 2nd of June. The captain, Mr. Bjarne, was aboard, and may have been somewhat astonished when his future passenger squeezed his hands violently in his joy. However, he took advantage of this eagerness to make us pay double fare—which fact did not affect my uncle at all.

'Come aboard on Tuesday, at seven in the morning,' said the captain, pocketing a very respectable number of dollars.

We thanked Mr. Thomsen for his kind help, and returned to the Phœnix.

'It's all going well! Very well!' repeated my uncle. 'What a fortunate chance to have found that boat nearly ready to sail! Now we'll have lunch, and see the town.'

We walked to the Kongens-Nye-Torw, an open space with two innocent cannons which could frighten nobody; there we found a French restaurant, where we lunched for the moderate sum of about two shillings each.

Then I took a youthful pleasure in strolling about the town; my uncle let me take him, but he saw nothing—neither the rather insignificant royal palace, nor the pretty seventeenth-century bridge which crosses the canal opposite the museum, nor the immense memorial to Thorwaldsen, containing some of his statues, but covered on the outside with hideous paintings, nor the Christmas-card castle of Rosenborg, in a quite pretty park, nor the Exchange, a fine Renaissance building, nor its bell-tower, made by the inter-laced tails of four bronze dragons, nor the great windmills on the ramparts, whose big sails filled like those of a ship with the sea-breeze.

How pleasant to have wandered there with Gräuben, but

alas! she was far away, and could I hope ever to see her again?

However, though my uncle cared nothing for these delightful scenes, he was much struck by a certain church-tower on the island of Amak, which forms the south-west quarter of Copenhagen.

I received the word of command to march in that direction; we embarked on a little steamer which plied on the canal, and soon reached the dockyard quay. After traversing some narrow streets where convicts, in striped grey and yellow garments, were working under supervision, we arrived at the Vor-Frelsers-Kirk. It was in no way remarkable except (and this is what had attracted my uncle) that an exterior staircase wound round and round the spire, up to the top.

'We will go up,' said my uncle.

'But we may get dizzy!' I answered.

'All the more reason.'

'But——'

'Come, boy, don't waste time.'

I had to obey. The custodian, who lived across the road, gave us the key, and the ascent began.

My uncle went first with a brisk step. I followed him in trepidation, for I was terribly subject to dizziness. However, as long as we were in the interior staircase, all went well; but after 150 steps the air blew upon my face—we had arrived at the platform of the tower. There the outer staircase began, protected only by a slender rail, and with steps which, growing ever narrower, seemed to reach up into the infinite.

'I couldn't possibly!' I cried.

'Am I to suppose you are a coward? Go on!' replied the pitiless professor.

I was forced to ascend, clinging to the rail. The open air stupefied me; I felt the spire sway in the wind; my legs gave way, and I found myself first progressing on my knees, and then *crawling* up! I closed my eyes, suffering from the fear of endless space.

At last, with my uncle's hand on my collar, I reached the terminal ball.

'Look,' he said, 'look down! You must take a lesson in contemplating the abyss!'

I was obliged to open my eyes. I saw the houses looking as if flattened out by a fall, in the midst of the smoke of their chimneys. Above my head were passing wisps of cloud, and by an optical illusion, to me they seemed motionless, while the spire, the ball, and I seemed to be carried along at a terrific speed. Far away, on the one side spread the verdant fields, on the other sparkled the sea under the sunbeams. The Sound extended to the Point of Elsinore, with a few white sails like seagulls' wings, and in the mist to eastwards the coast of Sweden was just distinguishable.

My uncle obliged me to stand up straight and look round. My first lesson in control of giddiness lasted an hour. When at last I was permitted to come down again and step on the solid pavement of the street, I could hardly walk upright.

'We'll do it again tomorrow,' said my professor.

And as a matter of fact, for five days I repeated this dizzying exercise, and in spite of myself I really made decided progress in the art of 'high contemplations'.

NINE

IN ICELAND

The day of our departure arrived. The day before, kind Mr. Thomsen had brought us cordial letters of recommendation to Count Trampe, governor of the island, Mr. Pictursson, the Bishop's coadjutor, and Mr. Finsen, the mayor of Reykjawik. In return, my uncle shook his hand with extreme heartiness.

On 2nd June, at six in the morning, our precious luggage was placed on board the *Valkyrie*, and the captain showed us to our somewhat narrow quarters.

'Is the wind favourable?' asked my uncle.

'Couldn't be better,' answered Captain Bjarne. 'A south-east wind. We shall leave the Sound with all sails set.'

A few minutes later we did so, and in an hour were passing the coast of Elsinore. In my nervous state of mind, I expected to see the ghost of Hamlet wandering on the celebrated terrace.

'Sublime madman!' I said, 'you would no doubt approve of us! You would like perhaps to follow us and seek the solution of your eternal problem in the centre of the earth!'

The *Valkyrie* was a fine sailer, but with a sailing-vessel one never can be quite sure what will happen. She was carrying to Reykjawik coal, household utensils, pottery, woollen clothes, and corn; the crew, all Danes, numbered only five.

Towards evening the schooner doubled Cape Skager, at the northern extremity of Denmark, traversed the Skager-rack in the night, skirted the southern point of Norway, the cape called The Naze, and gained the North Sea.

Two days after, we were in sight of Peterhead on the coast of Scotland, and then we passed between the Orkneys and Shetlands on our way to the Faroe Islands. On reaching these we steered a straight course for Cape Portland on the south coast of Iceland.

The voyage passed without incident; I managed to keep sea-sickness at bay, but my uncle, to his great annoyance and greater shame, succumbed completely to it.

He was therefore unable to question the captain about Snaefells, means of communication, and facilities for transport; all this had to be left till we landed.

On the 11th we passed Cape Portland, and saw the Myrdals Jokul which dominates it. The *Valkyrie* then proceeded westwards, at a fair distance from the coast, amidst shoals of whales and sharks. Soon we saw an immense rock tunnelled right through, and furious waves rushing through the gap. The Westman Isles seemed to be floating on the liquid sea. From thence the schooner gave herself sea-room in doubling Cape Reykjaness, which forms the south-western angle of the island.

Forty-eight hours later, after a storm which forced us to reef all sail, we sighted the buoy on the dangerous Skagen Point. An Icelandic pilot came aboard, and three hours later the *Valkyrie* anchored in the bay of Faxa, off Reykjawik.

The pale but undaunted professor came out of his cabin

at last; and the population of the town gathered on the quay, intensely interested in a vessel which was bringing something for each of them.

My uncle hastened to leave his floating prison, but before doing so he pointed out to me, to northwards, a high mountain with two points, a double cone covered with perpetual snow. 'Snaefells!' he cried, 'Snaefells!'

Then, with a gesture enjoining absolute silence, he climbed down into the rowing-boat which took us to the shore of Iceland. The Governor, Mr. Trampe, at once appeared; my uncle handed him the letter from Copenhagen, and a short conversation in Danish took place, in which I took no part, for a sufficient reason. But the upshot of it was that the Governor was entirely at the disposal of Professor Lidenbrock.

Mr. Finsen, the mayor, was also very kind, but Mr. Pictursson, the Bishop's coadjutor, was making a pastoral tour in the island. However, we met a delightful and most helpful man, Mr. Fridriksson, teacher of natural science at the Reykjawik school. He only spoke Icelandic and Latin, but he and I got on very well together in the latter language.

This good man installed us in two out of the three rooms composing his house, and my uncle said to me: 'Now the most difficult part is done!'

'The most difficult?' said I.

'Certainly,' he answered. 'Once we're there, we only have to go down!'

'But what about coming up again?'

'Oh! don't worry about *that*. Come, there's no time to lose. I'm going to the library; they may have some manuscript of Saknussemm's, and if so I should like to consult it.'

For my part, I preferred to wander through the town, without fear of losing my way, in spite of my ignorance of the language, for there are only two streets. The longer runs parallel with the shore, and contains the houses of the merchants and shopkeepers, built of red wooden beams laid horizontally; the other road, more to the west, leads to a little lake, and on each side are the houses of the Bishop and some other non-commercial personages. Here also I found the cemetery, the Governor's house, the church built of blocks of lava, and on a neighbouring hill the State school, where as I was told later, the pupils are taught Hebrew, English, French, and Danish, four languages of which I, to my shame, am entirely ignorant.

The smaller houses are mere huts made of earth and peat, with their walls sloping so that they seem only roofs resting on the ground. But these roofs are fields. Owing to the warmth within, grass grows on them much better than in the cold ground, and at the haymaking time they are carefully mown, otherwise the animals would certainly seek their pasture on the verdant house-tops.

On my return, I found most of the population occupied in drying, salting, and packing cod, their principal export. The men seemed strong but heavy, fairer than Germans, pensive-looking, as if they felt themselves almost out of touch with humanity. They laughed occasionally, but I never saw one smile.

Their dress consisted of a jersey made of a coarse black wool known as *vadmel*, a broad-brimmed hat, trousers with a red stripe, and a piece of leather folded to form a foot-covering.

The women, with sad and resigned faces, pleasant, but wanting in vivacity, wore a bodice and petticoat of dark-

coloured *vadmel*; the girls had their hair plaited and sur-
mounted by a knitted cap of brown wool; the married
women covered their heads with a coloured handkerchief,
above which again appeared a piece of white linen.

After a good walk, I returned to find my uncle in company
with our host.

TEN

A DINNER IN ICELAND

Dinner was ready; my uncle did justice to it, after his compulsory fasting on the ship. The meal, which was rather Danish than Icelandic, was not remarkable in itself; but our host, more Icelandic than Danish, reminded me of tales of the hospitality of old. We were evidently to be made more at home than he was himself.

The conversation was in Icelandic, but my uncle put in some German and Mr. Fridriksson some Latin, so that I should understand. It was chiefly on scientific topics, but with complete reserve, on my uncle's part, as to our own projects.

Mr. Fridriksson at once inquired as to the upshot of my uncle's researches at the library.

'Your library!' cried the latter. 'There are only a few odd books on almost empty shelves!'

'Well,' replied his host, 'we have eight thousand volumes, many of which are precious and rare.'

'I don't know how you make that out,' said the professor. 'By my reckoning——'

'Oh! Mr. Lidenbrock, they are mostly out; the people of our old icy island are fond of study! Farmers and fishermen can read and do read. So these volumes, instead of mouldering behind a grating, are passing from hand to hand; they are read and re-read, and often return to the shelf only after an absence of a year or two.'

'Meanwhile,' said my uncle with some little annoyance, 'strangers——'

'But after all, strangers have their own libraries, and what matters most is that our peasants should receive instruction. We have actually a Literary Society which publishes books, and which has distinguished foreign correspondents. If you would become one, Mr. Lidenbrock, we should be honoured.'

My uncle, who already belonged to at least a hundred scientific societies, accepted with a good grace which touched Mr. Fridriksson.

'Now,' he said, 'tell me any book you were looking for, and I might help in finding it.'

After a little hesitation, my uncle said: 'Have you amongst the ancient books anything by Arne Saknussemm?'

'You mean the sixteenth-century man, a great naturalist alchemist, and traveller?'

'Exactly.'

'One of the glories of Icelandic literature and science? A very illustrious man?'

'As you say.'

'And whose courage matched his genius?'

'Just so; I see you know him well.' My uncle's eyes were sparkling as he added: 'Have you his works?'

'No, they are not to be had.'

'Not in Iceland?'

'Neither in Iceland nor anywhere else.'

'Why is that?'

'Because Arne Saknussemm was persecuted as a heretic, and in 1573 his works were burnt by the hangman at Copenhagen.'

'Good—excellent!' cried my uncle, to the horror of the Icelandic professor.

'I beg your pardon?' said the latter.

'Yes, that explains everything; I see why Saknussemm, proscribed and forced to conceal his discoveries, should have been obliged to hide his secret in a cryptogram——'

'What secret?' asked Mr. Fridriksson with interest.

'Oh, nothing really! I was only making a supposition—a pure supposition,' stammered my uncle.

'I see,' said Mr. Fridriksson, too polite to insist. 'I hope,' he added, 'that you will examine some of the mineral deposits of our island. There have been others before you, but they will not have exhausted the field. For instance, to go no farther, there is that mountain you see from here—Snaefells—one of the most interesting of volcanoes, with a crater which is seldom visited.'

'Is it extinct?'

'Oh yes, for five hundred years.'

'Well,' said my uncle, who was crossing his legs in a frenzied effort to keep himself from leaping up, 'I think I should like to begin my geological researches with that Seffel—Sneffel—what was it?'

'Snaefells,' repeated good Mr. Fridriksson.

This part of the conversation had been in Latin, so I understood, and I could hardly keep my countenance as I saw my uncle's vain attempts to conceal his elation.

'Yes,' he said, 'what you tell me decides me to climb the mountain, and perhaps even study the crater!'

'I am very sorry,' answered Mr. Fridriksson, 'that my duties will not allow me to accompany you; it would have given me both pleasure and profit.'

'Oh no! no! Mr. Fridriksson,' cried my uncle; 'of course

your duties come first, though your great knowledge would have been most useful to us.'

I can but hope that our simple Icelandic host did not see through my uncle's awkward expressions. At any rate he gave him instructions about the journey to Snaefells, which was to be by land, in default of a suitable boat to take us across the bay, and informed him of a trustworthy man, usually engaged in shooting eider-duck, who was coming there the next day, and who could probably be retained as a guide. He had the advantage of speaking Danish well.

The dinner ended with the heartiest thanks from the German to the Icelandic professor. The former had now learnt most important things, amongst others the history of Saknussemm, the reason for the mystery of the document, that his host would not be able to accompany us, and that tomorrow we should be able to obtain a guide.

ELEVEN

OUR GUIDE, HANS BJELKE

In the evening I took a short walk on the shore, and went to bed early on a bed of broad planks, sleeping profoundly.

When I awoke, I heard my uncle talking lengthily in the next room. I got up at once and hastened to join him.

He was talking in Danish with a tall and vigorous-looking man—one who gave the impression of unusual strength. His simple and intelligent eyes were set in a big head, and were of a dreamy blue colour. Long hair, which would be called red even in England, fell on his athletic shoulders. The Icelander was supple in his movements, but quiet, not given to gesticulation. His temperament seemed to be absolutely calm, though by no means indolent. One realized that he asked for nothing, worked as it suited him, and had a philosophy which preserved him from being either astonished or worried by the happenings of this world.

I observed these characteristics, as the man listened to my uncle's passionate eloquence. He remained with his arms folded, motionless before the wild gesticulations of the other; for the negative, his head turned from left to right; for the affirmative, it bent forward—and that so slightly, that his long hair scarcely moved. It was an economy of motion carried to the point of avarice.

Certainly I should never have guessed that this was a man who followed the chase; he would certainly not startle the game, but how could he reach it?

I understood better when Mr. Fridriksson explained to me how 'eiderdown' is obtained. The eider-duck is a pretty bird which builds its nest in early summer amongst the rocks of the numerous fjords; when complete, she lines it with the fine feathers which she plucks from her breast. Then the huntsman, or rather the merchant, arrives and takes the nest, and the poor duck begins all over again; and that goes on as long as she has any down left. When she is quite bare, the drake takes his turn; but as his feathers are hard and coarse and have no market value, his nest is not stolen, but left in peace. The duck lays her eggs, the young hatch out, and next year, the eiderdown harvest is again gathered.

Now as the eider-duck does not select steep rocks to build its nest, but rather those easy, horizontal ones which run out to sea, the 'huntsman' has a comparatively simple task.

The name of this grave, calm, and silent man was Hans Bjelke, and he was to be our guide.

His ways formed a great contrast with those of my uncle, but they got on well together. Neither thought much about terms—the one was ready to accept what was offered, the other to offer what was asked, so that the bargain was soon concluded.

Hans engaged to guide us to the village of Stapi, on the south side of the peninsula of Snaefells, at the very foot of the volcano. The distance by land, he said was about twenty-two miles, which my uncle reckoned to accomplish in two days, until he discovered that Danish miles were more than four of our miles! Thus we prepared for seven or eight days' march.

We were to have four ponies—one each for my uncle and myself, and two for the luggage. Hans would go on foot, as his habit was, and promised to take us the shortest way.

His engagement did not end at Stapi; he would continue to assist in our researches for the remuneration of three rixdollars (about 13*s*.) a week, but it was expressly stipulated that this should be paid down every Saturday evening.

The start was fixed for 16th June, and Hans retired.

'A splendid man,' cried my uncle, 'but he little knows what wonders are in store for him.'

'He is coming with us to——'

'The centre of the earth, Axel.'

During the forty-eight hours which remained we carefully arranged our effects into four groups, thus:

The instruments, comprising:

1. A centigrade thermometer, reading up to 150°, which seemed to me too high or too low. If the temperature of the air rose to that, we should be killed; but if it was to take the temperature of super-heated water or melted materials, it was insufficient.

2. A manometer of compressed air, to indicate pressures higher than that of the atmosphere at sea-level; an ordinary barometer would not have sufficed.

3. A chronometer made by Boisonnas, of Geneva, regulated at the longitude of Hamburg.

4. Two compasses, one for inclination, the other for declination or dip.

5. Two electric lamps, worked by Ruhmkorff coils.

The arms consisted of two rifles, two revolvers, and a considerable amount of gun-cotton, unaffected by damp.

The tools comprised two picks, two mattocks, a ladder of silk rope, three iron-shod staves, a hatchet, a hammer, some nuts and screws, some long knotted cords. That made a good big package, for the ladder was three hundred feet long.

Lastly, there were the provisions—not a large package, but satisfactory, for I knew that in concentrated meat and biscuits there was enough for six months. The only liquid was gin—no water, but we had our flasks, and the fears I expressed to my uncle as to the quality and temperature of the water we should find, if we found any, were totally disregarded.

I ought also to add that we had a travelling medicine-chest containing blunt scissors, bandages, and bleeding-apparatus (rather alarming!), also bottles of dextrin, spirits of wine, lead acetate, ether, vinegar and ammonia, and the necessary chemicals for the Ruhmkorff coils.

My uncle had carefully remembered to provide tobacco, gunpowder, and tinder, also a leather belt which he wore round his body and which contained a good sum in gold, silver, and notes. There were six pairs of good boots, water-proofed with rubber and tar, along with the tools.

On the 14th we dined with the Governor, in company with the mayor and the principal doctor. I understood nothing of the conversation. On the 15th we completed our preparations, and received from our host a map of Iceland far superior to our own, on a scale of 1 : 480,000, which delighted my uncle.

After an agitated night, at least on my part, I was awakened by the neighing of horses, and saw Hans, who had just loaded up our luggage without moving, so to speak, but with wonderful skill. By six o'clock all was ready; we shook hands with Mr. Fridriksson, and my uncle thanked him very warmly for his kindly hospitality. I said what I could in Latin, and as we started, Mr. Fridriksson repeated Vergil's line: '*Et quacunque viam dederit fortuna sequamur.*'

TWELVE

ON THE WAY TO SNAEFELLS

The day was cloudy but fine—a good day for travelling, without risk of either excessive heat or rain.

The pleasure of riding through an unknown country gave me a good start; I gave myself up to the joy of the tourist, compounded of desires and liberty. I began to take my part in the expedition.

'Besides,' I said to myself, 'what risks am I running? That of travelling through a most interesting country, ascending a very remarkable mountain, possibly going down to the bottom of the crater of an extinct volcano? Evidently that is what Saknussemm did. As to the existence of a passage leading to the centre of the globe, it's pure imagination! Pure impossibility! So I'll take all the good in this expedition without worrying.'

We had now left Reykjawik. Hans walked ahead, with a rapid, equal, and untiring step. The two baggage-ponies followed him of themselves, and then came my uncle and I, looking not too ridiculous on our small but hardy beasts.

Iceland is one of the largest islands in Europe; it has an area of fourteen thousand square miles, but has a population of only sixty thousand. Geographers divide it into four quarters, and we had to traverse obliquely the one called the south-west quarter.

Hans, on leaving Reykjawik, had immediately taken to a coast path; we rode between meagre pastures which had much trouble to be green—there was a good deal of yellow in the colour. The rugged summits of the trachytic hills on the horizon were rendered indefinite by the mist to eastward; at times sheets of snow, concentrating the diffused light, gleamed brightly on the sides of far-off mountains; some sheer peaks clove the grey clouds and appeared again above the moving vapours, like reefs in the seas of heaven.

Often these chains of arid rocks formed promontories extending towards the sea, and encroaching on the pasturages, but there was always sufficient room to pass. Besides, our horses always chose by instinct the best way without slackening their pace. My uncle had not even the consolation of urging his mount on with voice or whip; he had no opportunity of being impatient. I could not help smiling on seeing how tall he looked on his little pony, and as his long legs brought his feet almost to the ground, he looked like a centaur with six legs.

'Good beast! Good beast!' he said. 'You'll see, Axel, there's no animal more intelligent than an Icelandic horse; snow, storms, impassable roads, rocks, glaciers—none of these can stop him. He is brave, quiet, and sure. Never a stumble, never a fit of nerves. If there is a river or a fjord to be crossed, and there will be, you will see him go into the water without hesitation, like an amphibian, and swim across. But don't let us worry him, let him alone, and we shall do our thirty miles a day.'

'*We* shall, I dare say,' I replied, 'but what about the guide?'

67

'Oh, I'm not anxious about him. These people walk almost mechanically; this man moves so little that he doesn't get tired. Besides, at need I can lend him my horse. I shall soon get cramped, if I don't exercise my limbs. The arms are all right, but one must think of one's legs.'

Meanwhile we made rapid progress; the country we passed through was already practically uninhabited. Here and there an isolated farm, some solitary *baer*, made of wood, earth, and blocks of lava, appeared like a beggar at the edge of a sunk lane. These miserable huts gave the impression of imploring charity from passers-by, and one felt inclined to offer them alms. In this region there were no roads, nor even paths, and the vegetation, however slowly it grew, had an easy task in obliterating the steps of the rare travellers.

And yet this part of the province, so near to the capital, counted as one of the populated and cultivated portions of Iceland. What then were the regions yet more deserted than this desert? We had not yet come across a farmer at the door of his cottage, nor a wild shepherd minding a flock less wild than himself; only some cows and sheep left to their own devices. What then would be the condition of the regions convulsed by eruptive phenomena, formed by volcanic explosions and subterranean disturbances?

We were destined to know them later; but consulting Olsen's map, I saw that they were avoided by following the sinuous edge of the coast; indeed, the great plutonic movement took place specially in the interior of the island; there the horizontal layers of the rock called trap, the beds of trachyte, the eruptions of basalt, tufa, and all the volcanic conglomerates, the streams of lava and fused porphyry, have created a land of supernatural horror. I had at that time no idea of the sight which awaited us on the peninsula of

Snaefells, where these vestiges of nature in commotion form a formidable chaos.

Two hours after having left Reykjawik we arrived at the little town of Gufunes, described as *aðalkirkja*, or seat of a principal church. It had only a few houses, and would be a mere hamlet in Germany.

Here Hans called a half-hour's halt; he shared our frugal meal, answered by yes and no my uncle's questions about the road, and when asked where he proposed to spend the night, answered with the one word 'Gardär'.

I consulted the map, and saw a village of that name on the shore of the Hvalfjord, about eighteen miles from Reykjawik. I showed it to my uncle.

'Eighteen miles!' he cried. 'Eighteen miles out of a hundred! That's a very poor distance!' He began to say something about it to the guide, who, without answering, led the horses forward and started again.

Three hours later, still travelling over the pale grass of the pasture-land, we rounded the Kollafjord, this process being less trouble than crossing it; soon we entered a *pingstaðer* or communal headquarters, called Ejulberg, from the church-tower of which noon would have sounded, had Icelandic churches been rich enough to have clocks; but they are like the members of their congregations, who have no watches, and do very well without.

There the horses were baited; thence we reached the *aðalkirkja* of Brantar, and at four in the afternoon were on the south side of the Hvalfjord, which at that point was about half a mile wide.

The waves were breaking noisily on sharp-edged rocks, and the sides of the fjord were walls of rock three thousand feet high composed of brown layers separated by beds of a reddish tufa. I did not look forward to crossing this arm of the sea on the back of a quadruped, and held back, but my uncle on the contrary pressed his pony on to the edge of the waves. The animal sniffed, refused to enter, and shook its head. There followed swearing and blows, met with plunging on the part of the pony, which finally, bending its limbs, escaped from under the professor, and left him standing on two rocks, like the Colossus of Rhodes!

'You accursed beast!' exclaimed his rider, suddenly transformed into a pedestrian.

'Ferja,' said the guide, touching him on the shoulder.

'What! A boat?'

'Der,' replied Hans, pointing to one.

'Yes,' I cried, 'there is a boat.'

'You should have said so then. Well, let us start!'

'Tidvatten,' replied the guide.

'What does that mean?' I asked.

'He says the tide,' said my uncle, translating the Danish word.

'I suppose we must wait for the tide?'

'Forbida?' asked my uncle.

'Ja,' replied Hans.

My uncle tapped with his foot, while the horses made their way towards the boat.

I quite understood the necessity of waiting for a certain state of the tide to undertake the passage of the fjord, that at which the tide is highest. Then there is neither flow nor ebb, and the boat is not liable to be carried either to the head of the fjord or out to sea.

The favourable time was not till six in the evening; my uncle and I, the guide, two rowers, and the four horses all took our places in a rather doubtful-looking sort of flat ferryboat. Accustomed as I was to the steam ferry-boats of the Elbe, I considered the oars of our boatmen a poor mechanical device. The passage took more than an hour, but was eventually safely accomplished.

Half an hour afterwards we reached the *aðalkirkja* of Gardär.

THIRTEEN

NEARING THE MOUNTAIN

It should have been night, but at the sixty-fifth degree of latitude I could not be astonished at the length of the polar day; in Iceland, during June and July, the sun never sets.

Still, the temperature had fallen; I was cold, and still more I was hungry. Welcome was the *baer* which opened hospitably to receive us.

It was a peasant's house, but in point of hospitality it was equal to a king's palace. On our arrival, the master shook hands with us, and without further ceremony made signs to us to follow him.

Indeed it would have been impossible to walk beside him. A long, narrow, dark passage led into the house, built of roughly-squared beams, and gave access to each of the four rooms—the kitchen, the workshop for weaving, the *badstofa* or family bedroom, and the best room of all, that for strangers. My uncle, whose stature had not been contemplated when the house was built, had the misfortune to knock his head three or four times against the beams of the ceiling.

We were shown into our room, a large apartment with a floor of beaten earth and a window in which the place of glass was taken by stretched sheep-membranes, not very transparent. The beds consisted of dry hay heaped into two frames of wood, painted red and adorned with Icelandic sayings. I did not expect so much comfort; only the house was pervaded with a smell of dried fish, pickled meat, and sour milk, to which my nose found it very difficult to accommodate itself.

When we had laid aside our travelling equipment, we heard the voice of our host, inviting us to come into the kitchen, the only room which had a fire, even in the most severe weather.

My uncle decided to obey this friendly injunction, and I followed him. It was a primitive hearth—a stone in the middle of the room, and a hole in the roof for the smoke to escape! The kitchen was also the dining-room.

At our entrance the host, as if he had not yet seen us, saluted us with the word *sœllvertu* which means 'Be happy', and came and kissed us on the cheek.

His wife next pronounced the same word, accompanied by the same ceremony; then the two, placing their right hands on their hearts, bowed low.

I hasten to add that the woman was the mother of nineteen children, who were all, big and little, crowded together amid the clouds of smoke with which the fire was filling the room. Every minute I observed some fair little head, with a rather melancholy expression, appearing out of the cloud. It reminded one of a circle of somewhat unwashed angels.

My uncle and I were very friendly to these nestlings, and soon there were two or three of them on our shoulders, as many on our knees, and the rest between them. Those who could speak repeated *sœllvertu* in every imaginable tone. Those who could not shouted all the louder.

This concert was interrupted by the announcement of the

73

meal. At this moment our guide returned, after seeing to the beasts, that is, taking the economical course of setting them free to find their own pasture; the poor beasts had to be content with cropping the scanty moss on the rocks, and some not very nourishing seaweeds; the next day they would not fail to return of their own accord to take up their labours.

'Sœllvertu,' said Hans on entering.

Then quietly, mechanically, without one kiss being warmer than another, he kissed the host, the hostess, and their nineteen children.

This ceremony ended, we sat down, to the number of twenty-four, and consequently one on the top of the other, in the literal sense of the words. The most favoured had only *two* little ones on his knees.

From the arrival of the soup there was silence in this little company, and the taciturnity natural to Icelanders, even in youth, resumed its sway. The host served out a soup made from lichen, by no means unpalatable, then an enormous portion of dried fish swimming in sour butter which was twenty years old, and therefore, according to Icelandic ideas, vastly preferable to fresh butter. With it there was *skyr*, a sort of curded milk, accompanied with biscuit and seasoned with the juice of juniper-berries; and for drink, milk and water, which they call *blanda*. Whether this peculiar meal was good or not, I am not in a position to decide. I only know that I was hungry, and ended by swallowing, down to the last spoonful, some thick buckwheat soup.

After the meal, the children disappeared; their elders assembled round the hearth, on which was a fire of peat, fern, cow-dung, and dry fish-bones. Then, after this 'warm-up' the different groups betook themselves to their respective rooms. The hostess offered, as was customary, to take off our stockings for us; but on meeting with a gracious refusal, did not insist, and I was at last able to snuggle down in my bed of hay.

Next day, at five o'clock, we bade farewell to the Iceland peasant; my uncle with great difficulty induced him to accept a suitable remuneration, and Hans gave the signal for departure.

At a hundred yards from Gardär, the ground began to change in appearance; it became marshy, and the going was more difficult. On the right, the range of mountains was indefinitely prolonged like an immense natural system of fortifications, the counterscarp of which we were following; often streams crossed our path which had to be forded without too much wetting of the baggage.

The solitude became more and more profound; but sometimes a human shadow appeared to be fleeing away, and when the windings of the road brought us unexpectedly near to one of these spectres, I experienced a sudden disgust at the sight of a swollen head with gleaming skin, without hair, and exhibiting repulsive sores through the rents in miserable rags.

The poor creature did not come and hold out his deformed hand; on the contrary he fled, but not so quickly as to prevent Hans from saluting him with the usual 'Sœllvertu'.

'Spetalsk,' explained he.

'A leper!' repeated my uncle.

And this word alone produced its effect of repulsion. This horrible infliction of leprosy is fairly common in Iceland; it is not contagious, but hereditary, so marriage is forbidden to these unfortunates.

These sights were not of a nature to adorn the landscape, which was becoming profoundly dreary; the last blades of grass were dying beneath our feet. There was not a tree,

apart from a few thickets of birches so dwarfed as to be rather bushes. Nor was there an animal, except some horses for which their owners had no food, and which had run wild on the desolate plains. Sometimes a hawk soared amongst the grey clouds, flying rapidly towards sunnier lands; I surrendered myself to the melancholy proper to this wild region, and memory carried me back to my native land.

After crossing several little fjords and one broad one, fortunately at a favourable state of the tide, we found ourselves obliged to pass the night in a deserted house, a fit abode for all the goblins of Scandinavian mythology; certainly the frost-fiend had his domicile there, and showed his power during the night.

The next day was uneventful—the same marshy ground,

the same monotony, the same dismal landscape. But that evening we had traversed half the distance to Snaefells, and we slept at Krösolbt.

On the 19th of June, for about a mile, a floor of lava lay beneath our feet; the wrinkles in the surface of this lava took the form of cables, sometimes stretched out, sometimes coiled up; there was an immense flow from the adjoining mountains, testifying to the former activity of these now extinct volcanoes. Even now some vapours rising here and there betrayed underground heat.

We had not time to examine into these phenomena; we had to press on. Soon the marshy ground, intersected by little lakes, re-appeared under our ponies' feet. Our direction now became due west—we had rounded the great bay of Faxa, and the white double crest of Snaefells appeared in the clouds hardly more than twenty miles away.

The horses went well, unhindered by the difficulty of the surface. As to me, I was beginning to feel very tired, but my uncle was as fresh and upright as on the first day, and I could not help admiring him as much as the guide, who looked upon the whole expedition as a little excursion.

On Saturday, 20th June, at six in the evening, we reached Büdir, a village on the coast, and Hans demanded his promised wages. My uncle settled with him. It was his own family, that is, his uncles and cousins, that offered us hospitality here; we were kindly received, and without wishing to impose on their goodwill, I would gladly have stayed with them a little to recover from the fatigues of the journey. But my uncle, having nothing to recover from, did not see things in that light, and next morning we once more bestrode our faithful beasts.

The ground betrayed the neighbourhood of the mountain,

its granite roots rising from the soil like those of an old oak. We were skirting the immense base of the volcano. The professor kept his gaze fixed on it, gesticulating, seeming to defy it, and to say:

'So that is the giant whom I am to overcome!'

At last the horses stopped of their own accord at the door of the parsonage at Stapi.

FOURTEEN

ARGUMENTS IN VAIN

Stapi is a village formed of thirty or so huts, built on lava and enjoying the rays of the sun reflected from the volcano. It extends to the head of a little fjord enclosed by a wall of an extraordinary appearance.

It is generally known that basalt is a brown rock of igneous origin; it takes forms which are surprising in their regularity. Here nature proceeds geometrically, working in human fashion, as if she were furnished with set square, compasses, and plumb-line. If elsewhere she uses with artistic effect masses flung in disorder, the beginnings of cones, imperfect pyramids, here, wishing to give an example of regularity, and anticipating our early architects, she has created severe order, unsurpassed by the splendours of Babylon or the marvels of Greece.

I had indeed heard tell of the Giant's Causeway in Ireland, and of Fingal's Cave in Staffa, but I had never yet beheld the spectacle of basaltic structure; now at Stapi this phenomenon appeared in all its beauty.

The sides of the fjord, and the whole coast of the peninsula, were composed of a succession of vertical columns, thirty feet high. These straight and well-proportioned pillars supported others laid horizontally and projecting beyond them so as to overhang the sea. At certain intervals, under this natural roof, one had a vision of beautiful arched gateways, through which the waves from the open sea rushed, breaking themselves in foam. Some fragments of basalt columns, broken off by the fury of the ocean, lay along the beach like the ruins of an antique temple, ruins eternally young, over which the centuries pass without effect.

Such was the last stage of our journey. Hans had guided us intelligently, and it reassured me a little to think that he would still be with us.

On arriving at the door of the rector's house, a simple low cabin, neither handsomer nor more comfortable than its neighbours, I saw a man shoeing a horse, with a hammer in his hand, and wearing a leather apron.

'Sœllvertu,' said the guide.

'God dag,' answered the blacksmith in perfect Danish.

'Kyrkoherde,' said Hans, turning to my uncle.

'The rector!' repeated the latter. 'It seems, Axel, that this good man is the rector.'

Meanwhile the guide explained the situation to the *kyrkoherde*; the latter, suspending his work, uttered a sort of cry which is no doubt familiar to horses and horse-dealers, and at once a tall woman with the look of a shrew came out of the hut. If she was not six feet high, she was certainly not far short of it.

I was afraid she would offer the travellers the usual Icelandic kiss; but she did not, and indeed was not too gracious in her invitation to enter.

The guest-room here seemed the worst in the rectory, small, dirty and evil-smelling. We had to put up with it— the rector did not seem to practise traditional hospitality— far from it. Before night, I saw that we were dealing with a

80

blacksmith, a fisherman, a hunter, a carpenter, but by no means a minister of the Lord. It is possible, however, that he was different on Sunday!

My uncle soon saw what he was like, and decided to press on in spite of fatigue, so the day after our arrival we prepared for the ascent of the mountain. Hans hired the services of three Icelanders to replace the horses in carrying our effects; but it was understood that, once arrived at the bottom of the crater, the natives would go home and leave us to ourselves.

On this occasion my uncle was obliged to confide to the guide his intention of exploring the depths of the volcano as far as he could possibly go.

Hans contented himself with nodding. To go to one place or another, to penetrate into the bowels of his island or to walk on its surface, was all one to him; I for my part had so far been distracted by the events of our journey, but now I was once more a prey to violent emotion. But what could I do? If any attempt at resisting Professor Lidenbrock had been possible, it should have been at Hamburg, not at the foot of Snaefells.

One idea of all others agitated me terribly, a most alarming idea, and one calculated to affect nerves even less sensitive than mine.

'Let me see,' I said, 'we are to climb Snaefells. Good. We are to descend into the crater. Good. Others have done so and survived. But that is not all. If we can discover a passage into the interior of the earth, if that accursed Saknussemm has spoken the truth, we shall lose ourselves amongst the subterranean galleries of the volcano. Now, how can we be sure that Snaefells is extinct? Who can prove that an eruption is not now in preparation? Because the monster has been asleep since 1229, does it follow that it will never awake again? And if it does, what will become of us?'

That seemed a subject for reflection, and I did reflect. I could not sleep without dreaming of eruptions; and I did not take easily to the idea of being cast up by one.

At last I could bear it no longer; I went and found my uncle, and put the case as a most improbable hypothesis, but I kept well away from him in case of an explosion.

'Yes, I was thinking of that,' he replied simply.

Could he be about to listen to reason, and give up his mad project? Or was that too good to be true? After a few minutes' silence, which I dared not break, he continued:

'I've thought of it. We must not be imprudent.'

'*No*,' I said emphatically.

'Snaefells has been quiet for six hundred years, but it *might* awake. Now eruptions are always preceded by well-known phenomena; so I have questioned the inhabitants and examined the ground, and I can assure you, Axel, that there will be no eruption.'

He then took me by a path which led inland, amid enormous rocks made of trap, basalt, granite, and other igneous materials. Here and there I saw fumaroles mounting into the air—columns of white steam called *reykir* in the Icelandic tongue, rising from hot streams and indicating, by their violence, the volcanic activity of the region. This seemed to me to justify my fears, so I was taken aback when my uncle said:

'You see, Axel, we have nothing to fear from the volcano. At the approach of an eruption these fumaroles redouble their activity, and then disappear altogether while it is in progress, for the imprisoned gases, the pressure being relieved, escape through the crater instead of making use of

82

these fissures. If these vapours then are in their usual condition, we may be sure that no eruption is at hand.'

'But——'

'Enough. When science has spoken, it behoves us to be silent.'

I returned to the rectory with a flea in my ear; my one hope now was that there would be no passage from the crater downwards, but that night I suffered from a fearful nightmare, in which I was in the depths of a volcano, from which I was shot forth into planetary space in the form of an erupted rock.

Next day, 23rd June, Hans was ready for us with his companions laden with the provisions, tools, and instruments. Two iron-shod sticks, two guns and cartridge-belts were reserved for my uncle and me. Hans, as a careful man, had added to our stores a leather bottle which, together with our flasks, assured us a week's water.

It was nine in the morning. The rector and his tall shrew were waiting at the door, no doubt to say the last farewell of the host to the traveller. But this farewell took the form of a formidable bill, in which nothing was forgotten. My uncle paid without bargaining; a man on his way to the centre of the earth does not look too closely at a few rixdollars.

The bill settled, Hans gave the signal for departure, and in a minute or two we had left Stapi.

FIFTEEN

THE SUMMIT OF SNAEFELLS

Snaefells is five thousand feet high; its double cone forms the extreme point of a band of trachyte which stands apart from the contour-system of the island. From our starting-point we could not see these two peaks outlined against the grey sky—all that was visible was an immense cowl of snow covering the giant's brow.

We walked in single file, the guide first; he went by narrow paths where two abreast could not pass. Thus conversation was almost impossible.

Beyond the basalt wall of the fjord of Stapi, there was at first a soil composed of fibrous peat, the remains of the former vegetation of the marshes. The quantity of this yet unused fuel would suffice to warm the whole population of Iceland for a century; this immense peat-bog, as estimated from the depth of certain ravines, was in places seventy feet thick, and showed successive layers of carbonized remains, separated by sheets of pumice or tufa.

The way became more and more difficult; we began to rise, and to set in motion loose stones which came clattering down, and were only evaded by the most scrupulous care.

Hans advanced peacefully as if on plain ground; sometimes he disappeared behind a great block and was lost to sight for a moment; then a shrill whistle from his lips told us in what direction to follow. Often too he stopped, collected some stones, and arranged them so as to form a landmark to help our return journey—a precaution good in itself, but one which future events rendered useless to us.

Three fatiguing hours' march had brought us only to the base of the mountain. There, Hans called a halt, and we made a hasty lunch. My uncle took double mouthfuls for the sake of speed; but as the halt was for the purpose of rest as well as nourishment, he was obliged to await the good pleasure of the guide, who started us again only after an hour. The three Icelanders, as silent as himself, said not a single word and ate temperately.

We now began to climb the slopes of Snaefells; its snow summit, by an optical effect common amongst mountains, appeared very close, and yet what long hours and what fatigue would be involved in reaching it! The stones, held together neither by earth nor grass, kept giving way under our feet, and rushing down to the plain with the speed of an avalanche.

In certain parts the slopes of the mountain made an angle of at least 36° with the horizontal; it was impossible to climb them, and we were obliged to skirt these steep, stony slopes, not without difficulty. At such places we helped each other by means of our poles.

I ought to say that my uncle kept as close to me as possible; he never lost sight of me, and many a time his arm gave me a strong support. As to himself, he evidently had an innate gift of equilibrium, for he never stumbled. The Icelanders, despite their burdens, climbed with the agility of the born mountaineer.

Seeing the height of the summit of Snaefells, it seemed to

me impossible to reach it from this side, unless the slope became less steep. Fortunately, after an hour of labours and difficult feats, in the midst of the great snow-sheet which covered the shoulder of the volcano, a sort of staircase appeared unexpectedly, and simplified our ascent. It was formed by one of those torrents of stones ejected by the eruptions, called *steinar* by the natives. If this one had not been stopped in its descent by the form of the mountain, it might have reached the sea and formed new islands.

Such as it was, it served us well; the steepness of the slope went on increasing, but these steps enabled us to ascend it easily, and indeed so rapidly that, having stayed behind for a minute while the others went on, I saw them already reduced by distance to a microscopic size.

At seven that evening we had ascended the two thousand steps of the 'stair', and were standing upon a sort of hump, from which, properly speaking, rose the cone which terminated in the crater.

The sea was spread out three thousand two hundred feet below; we were above the snow-line, which is not high in that latitude and so damp a climate. It was terribly cold, and there was a strong wind. I was exhausted; the professor saw that my legs were failing me, and in spite of his impatience, made up his mind to stop. He signed to the guide to that effect, but the latter shook his head, saying 'Ofvanför'.

'It seems we must go up higher,' said my uncle.

Then he asked Hans the reason for his decision.

'Mistour,' replied the guide.

'Ja, mistour,' repeated one of the Icelanders in a tone of alarm.

'What does that word mean?' I asked anxiously.

'Look,' said my uncle.

I looked towards the plain, and saw an immense column of powdered pumice-stone, sand, and dust rising and twirling like a water-spout; the wind was driving it against the side of Snaefells on which we were engaged; this opaque screen between us and the sun threw a great shadow on the mountain. If this column were to incline our way, we should inevitably be caught up in its eddies. This phenomenon, fairly common when the wind blows from the glaciers, is called in the Icelandic tongue 'mistour'.

'Hastigt, hastigt!' cried our guide. Without any knowledge of Danish, I understood that we were to follow Hans as fast as possible. The guide began to skirt the cone, but spirally, so as to make the ascent easier; soon the dust-storm struck the mountain with a shock which made it tremble; the stones lifted by the eddying winds rained down upon the earth as in an eruption. We were now, fortunately, on the opposite side and out of reach of danger; but for the precaution of our guide, however, our mangled bodies, reduced to dust, would have fallen afar off like the remains of some unknown meteorite.

Still, Hans thought it unwise to pass the night on the side of the cone. We continued our zigzag ascent; the fifteen hundred feet which remained to traverse took nearly five hours. Allowing for windings, the distance was at least nine miles, and I was utterly exhausted, succumbing to cold and hunger, while the rarefied air did not suffice to fill my lungs.

At last, at eleven o'clock at night, about the darkest time, the summit of Snaefells was reached, and before taking shelter within the crater, I had time to see the midnight sun at the lowest point of its course, casting its pale rays on the sleeping island.

SIXTEEN

IN THE CRATER

Supper was rapidly devoured, and the little party ensconced itself as best it could. The couch was hard, the shelter insufficient, and the situation unpleasant, five thousand feet above sea-level. And yet my sleep was particularly peaceful that night, better than for many previous ones. I did not even dream.

Next day we awoke almost frozen by the sharpness of the air, but in bright sunshine. I rose from my granite bed, and went to enjoy the magnificent spectacle which lay before my eyes.

I was at the summit of one of the peaks of Snaefells, the more southerly. Thence the view extended over the greater part of the island; the optical effect observed at all great heights made the horizon higher than it should be, while the central portions were correspondingly depressed. One would have said that one of Helbesmer's relief-maps was spread at my feet; I saw deep valleys meeting one another in all directions, precipices dug out like wells, lakes appearing as ponds, and rivers as streams. On my right was a succession of innumerable glaciers and a forest of peaks, some of which were crested with faint smoke-wreaths. The undulations of this infinite series of mountains, with their foamlike patches of snow, reminded me of the surface of a stormy sea. When I turned towards the west the ocean was displayed in all its majestic extent, and seemed to continue the waves of the mountains. The line where the land ended and the sea began was barely distinguishable to the eye.

I lost myself in the ecstasy proper to great peaks, and this time without giddiness, for I was at last accustomed to such sublime contemplation. My dazzled gaze plunged into the midst of the transparent rays of the sun, I forgot who and where I was, and shared the life of the elves and sylphs of Scandinavian mythology; I was intoxicated by the excitement of altitude, disregarding the abysses into which my fate was soon to cast me. But I was brought back to the consciousness of reality by the arrival of the professor and Hans, who joined me on the summit of the peak.

My uncle, turning to the west, indicated with his hand a light vapour, mist, or faint outline of land which rose above the sea-line.

'Greenland,' he said.

'Greenland?' I cried.

'Yes, we are only about 105 miles away, and during thaws, Polar bears come thence to Iceland, carried on icebergs. But that doesn't concern us. We are at the top of Snaefells; here are the two peaks, this to the south, the other to the north. Hans will tell us what the Icelanders call the one on which we now stand.'

The question having been put, the guide replied: 'Scartaris'.

My uncle glanced at me in triumph.

'To the crater!' he said.

The crater of Snaefells was an inverted hollow cone with an opening about a mile and a half across. Its depth I estimated at about two thousand feet. One may guess the condition of a vessel of this capacity, when filled with thunder and flames! The bottom of the funnel would not measure more than five hundred feet round, so that the slope was fairly gentle, allowing of easy access to the lower part. I was involuntarily reminded by this crater of a great widened-out blunderbuss, and the comparison alarmed me.

'To go down into a blunderbuss,' I thought, 'when it is perhaps loaded, and may go off at the least touch, is the act of a madman.'

But I could not go back. Hans, with an air of indifference, led the party again. I followed without a word.

To facilitate the descent, Hans described very elongated ellipses in the interior of the cone; we were walking in the midst of erupted rocks, some of which, shaken in their sockets, were dashed down, bounding and rebounding, to the bottom of the abyss. Their fall produced reverberating echoes, strangely sonorous.

There were actually glaciers at some parts of the interior of the cone; across them Hans advanced only with extreme caution, sounding with his iron staff to discover crevasses. At certain doubtful points it became necessary to tie us with a long cord, so that if anyone unexpectedly slipped, he would be held up by his companions. This precaution was a prudent one, but it did not exclude all risk.

In spite, however, of all the difficulties of the descent on slopes which were new to the guide himself, it was accomplished without accident, except for the loss of a packet of cords which slipped from the hands of one of the porters, and took the shortest way to the bottom of the abyss.

At noon we had arrived. I raised my head, and saw the upper opening of the cone forming a greatly reduced but almost perfect circular disc of sky. Only at one point rose the peak of Scartaris, piercing the heavens.

At the bottom of the crater there appeared three channels, through which at the time of the eruptions of Snaefells, the central furnace must have belched forth its lava and steam. Each of these was somewhere about a hundred feet across. They were there yawning under our feet. Professor Lidenbrock at once rapidly examined their respective positions; he was panting, rushing from one to the other, gesticulating and stammering forth unintelligible words. Hans and his companions, seated on blocks of lava, watched him, and evidently believed him to be out of his mind.

Suddenly my uncle uttered a cry; I thought he had lost his footing and was falling into one of the three openings. But

no, I saw him standing with arms extended and legs apart, upright before a granite rock in the centre of the crater, which resembled an enormous pedestal for a statue of Pluto. He was in an attitude of stupefaction, but this soon gave way to immeasurable joy.

'Axel! Axel!' he cried, 'come, come!'

I hastened to him. Neither Hans nor the Icelanders stirred.

'Look,' said the professor.

And, sharing in his astonishment, if not in his joy, I read on the western face of the block, in runic characters partly worn away by time, the thrice-accursed name

ᛉᛐᛏᛏᚢᛑᛑᛐᛐᛏ ᛏᛐᛑᛐ

'Arne Saknussemm!' cried my uncle; 'can you have any doubts *now*?'

I made no answer, but returned in consternation to my lava seat, overwhelmed by this piece of evidence.

I cannot say how long I remained absorbed in reflection. All I know is that when I raised my head I saw only my uncle and Hans at the bottom of the crater. The Icelanders had been dismissed, and were now descending the outer slopes of Snaefells on their way back to Stapi.

Hans was sleeping peacefully at the foot of a rock, in a lava-stream from which he had improvised a bed; my uncle was circling about the bottom of the crater like a wild beast in the pit made by a trapper. I had neither desire nor strength to rise, and following the example of the guide, I abandoned myself to a miserable kind of drowsiness, through which I seemed to hear sounds or feel tremblings in the depths of the mountain.

Thus passed the first night at the bottom of the crater.

Next day a grey, cloudy, heavy sky hung over the summit of the cone. I noticed it not so much by the darkness within as by the intense annoyance of my uncle.

I understood the reason for this, and my heart felt a returning ray of hope.

Of the three opening beneath us, one only was that of Saknussemm. According to the Icelandic sage, it was to be known by the circumstance mentioned in the cryptogram, that the shadow of Scartaris fell on its margin during the last days of the month of June. One might in fact consider this sharp peak as an immense sundial, the shadow of which on a given day indicated the route to the centre of the earth.

Now, if the sunshine failed, there would be no shadow, and consequently no guide. It was 25th June. If the sky would only remain dull for six days, the observation would have to be postponed for another year!

I refrain from depicting the helpless fury of Professor Lidenbrock. The day wore on, and no shadow appeared on the bottom of the crater. Hans did not stir from his place, though he must have wondered why we were waiting, if he ever wondered! My uncle did not speak a word to me. His gaze, perpetually turned towards the sky, was lost in its grey and cloudy depths.

On the 26th, still no sun, and sleet fell all day. Hans built a hut with blocks of lava. It gave me some pleasure to follow with my eye the thousands of little sudden cataracts on the sides of the cone, making a deafening sound echoed by every stone.

My uncle could no longer contain himself. It was enough to irritate a more patient man, for this was veritably shipwreck within sight of land.

But heaven is apt to mingle great joys with great griefs, and it held in store for Professor Lidenbrock a piece of satisfaction to match his desperate anxiety.

The next day the sky was still cloudy, but on Sunday, 28th June, the last day but one of the month, with the change of the moon came a change in the weather. The sun cast floods of light into the crater. Each little mound, each rock, each stone, each mere roughness, sharing in the beneficent rays, instantly cast its shadow on the ground. Above all, that of Scartaris showed as a clear-cut ridge, slowly travelling with the radiant orb.

My uncle turned with it.

At noon, when at its shortest, the shadow gently caressed the edge of the central opening.

'There!' cried the professor, 'that's the way! To the centre of the globe!' he added in Danish.

I looked at Hans.

'Forüt!' said the guide tranquilly.

'Forward!' replied my uncle. It was 1.13 p.m.

SEVENTEEN

THE REAL JOURNEY BEGINS

The real journey was beginning. Up till now we had experienced labours rather than difficulties; now the latter were to spring up at every step.

I had not yet gazed down into the bottomless well into which I was to be plunged, but the moment had now come. I could still either take my part in the enterprise or refuse to attempt it. But I was ashamed to draw back in the presence of the guide. Hans was accepting the adventure so quietly, with such indifference, such a total disregard of danger, that I blushed at the thought of being less brave than he was. Alone, I might have brought forward a great array of arguments; but in the company of Hans I was silent. I called up a memory of my pretty Gräuben, and approached the central chimney.

I have said that it was about a hundred feet across, or three hundred feet round. I leaned over a projecting rock, and looked down—my hair stood on end! The horror of the void seized on me. I felt my centre of gravity moving, and vertigo mounting to my head like intoxication. There is nothing more irresistible than the attraction of the abyss. I was about to fall, but a hand restrained me; it was that of

95

Hans. It was evident I had not taken quite enough lessons at the church in Copenhagen.

However, though I had not looked long into the chimney, I had seen very well what it was like. The walls, almost vertical, nevertheless presented numerous projections which would serve as footholds; but if the stairs were not wanting, the hand-rail was entirely to seek! A rope fastened up above would have answered, but how could we detach it, when arrived at the lower end?

My uncle got over this difficulty in a very simple way. He unwound a rope about a thumb's thickness and four hundred feet long; first he let down half of it, then made a loop over a firm projecting block of lava, and then sent the other half down. Thus we could each descend by holding on to both halves of the cord; when we were all about two hundred feet down, nothing would be simpler than to regain our cord by letting go of one half and pulling on the other. This process could be repeated *ad infinitum*.

'Now,' said my uncle after having finished these arrangements, 'let us see about the baggage; it must be divided into three packages, and each of us must carry one on his back—only fragile objects, I mean.' (The bold professor evidently did not include *ourselves* under this heading.) 'Hans,' he said, 'will take charge of the tools and some of the provisions. You, Axel, of a second portion of provisions, and the guns; myself, of the rest of the food, and the delicate instruments.'

'But,' I said, 'what about the clothes, and all these ropes and ladders?'

'They will go by themselves.'

'What do you mean?' I asked in astonishment.

'You will see.'

My uncle was given to employing drastic measures, and

never hesitated. At his order, Hans roped together the non-fragile things, and simply threw the package down the chimney!

I heard the loud rushing sound produced by the displacement of layers of air. My uncle, leaning over the depth, followed the descent of his belongings with a satisfied gaze, and only stood up when they were lost to view.

'Good,' he said. 'Our turn now.'

Let any honest man tell me if it was possible to hear such words without a shudder!

The professor took the packet of instruments on his back, Hans the tools, and I the guns. The descent began, in the following order—Hans, my uncle, myself. It took place in profound silence, disturbed only by the fall of pieces of rock into the depths.

I let myself down, frantically clutching the double cord with one hand, with the other steadying myself by means of my iron-shod staff. A single idea dominated me—the fear that there should be no foothold somewhere. The rope seemed to me very inadequate for the weight of three persons. I used it as little as possible, performing miracles of balancing on the projecting blocks of lava, my feet doing their best to hold on like hands.

When one of these slippery steps gave way under Hans, he said in his quiet way, 'Gif akt!'

'Take care!' repeated my uncle.

In half an hour we had reached the surface of a rock firmly wedged into the wall of the chimney.

Hans pulled the cord at one end; the other flew up, and after passing the projecting rock above, came down, bringing with it a dangerous sort of rain, or rather hail, of loose stones.

Looking over the edge of our little platform, I could still perceive no bottom.

The manœuvre with the rope was repeated, and in another half-hour we had again descended two hundred feet. My uncle observed that the nature of the rocks confirmed him in his belief in Sir Humphry Davy's theory, and therefore in his doubts as to the central heat of the earth.

At the end of three hours, there was still no bottom visible; the orifice above was very much diminished and the light had almost gone.

Still we went on down, and I thought the sound made by the falling stones indicated that they were reaching the bottom sooner. By counting the number of times we had used the rope, I could calculate the depth reached, and also the time. We had repeated the operation fourteen times, and each took half an hour, so that made seven hours, plus fourteen quarters of an hour for rest, i.e. ten hours and a half altogether. We had started at one o'clock, so it must now be past eleven. And as the rope was two hundred feet long, the depth was two thousand eight hundred feet.

At this moment Hans called, 'Halt!'

I stopped just as I was about to step on my uncle's head.

'We have arrived,' he said.

'Where?' I asked, slipping down beside him.

'At the bottom of the perpendicular chimney.'

'But is there no way out!'

'Yes, I can just see a sort of passage slanting down to the right. We'll see about it tomorrow. First we'll have supper and then sleep.'

There was still a little light. We opened the bag of provisions, ate, and slept as well as we could on a bed of stones and pieces of lava.

Lying on my back, I looked up, and saw a brilliant speck at the end of the three-thousand-feet tube, which acted like an enormous telescope. It was a star.

Then I fell into a deep sleep.

EIGHTEEN

10,000 FEET BELOW SEA-LEVEL!

At eight in the morning we were awakened by a glint of day-light, reflected and broken up into a rain of bright sparks by the thousands of facets of the lava walls above. It was bright enough to enable us to distinguish the surrounding objects.

'Well, Axel, what do you say to it all?' said my uncle, rubbing his hands. 'Have you ever passed a more peaceful night at home? No noise of carts, or street cries, or boatmen's shouts!'

'Certainly it is quiet enough at the bottom of this well; quiet enough to be alarming!'

'Come,' said my uncle, 'we have not yet penetrated one inch into the bowels of the earth!'

'What *do* you mean?'

'We are just about at sea-level now.'

'Are you sure?'

'Quite sure; look at the barometer yourself.'

It was indeed true that the mercury, which had been rising as we descended, had stopped at twenty-nine inches.

'You see,' said my uncle, 'we have as yet only the pressure of one atmosphere; I am longing for the time when we shall have to replace the barometer by the manometer.'

'But,' I said, 'will not this increased pressure be very painful to us?'

'No. We shall descend slowly, and so get used to it.'

At this moment Hans, pointing upwards, said, 'Der huppe!'

He was indicating the package which we had thrown down, and which had lodged on a projection a little above us. The agile Icelander climbed like a cat, and in a few minutes our package was returned to us.

'Now,' said my uncle, 'let us breakfast, remembering that we have a long journey before us.'

We partook of biscuits, meat, and some draughts of water with a little gin in it.

My uncle examined his instruments and took the following notes:

Monday, 29th June

Chronometer: 8 h. 17 m. in the morning.
Barometer: 29 inches, 7 lines.
Thermometer: 6°.
Direction: E.S.E.

This last observation, obtained from the compass, referred to the dark gallery upon which we were to enter.

'*Now*,' said my uncle, 'our journey is really beginning.'

So saying, he took in one hand the Ruhmkorff coil suspended from his neck; with the other he connected it with the filament of the lamp, and a very fair light penetrated the darkness of the gallery.

'Forward!' he cried. Each of us took up his burden; Hans came second, pushing before him the package of ropes and clothes, and I third, with one last glance upward through the immense tube, at that sky of Iceland which I should never see again.

At the last eruption, that of 1229, the lava had made its way through this tunnel. It had coated the interior with a smooth, shining layer, which reflected the electric light, multiplying its beams.

Our whole difficulty consisted in not slipping too rapidly down a slope of about 45°; fortunately certain irregularities served us as steps, and we had only to go on, letting our baggage, held by a long cord, slide down too.

But the substance which formed steps under our feet appeared as stalactites on the walls; the lava, porous in certain parts, formed little rounded blisters; crystals of opaque quartz, studded with smaller transparent ones, and suspended from the roof like chandeliers, seemed to light up as we passed. It might be said that the genii of the depths were illuminating their palace for the reception of guests from the surface.

'It's magnificent!' I cried involuntarily. 'What a sight, Uncle!'

'Ah, you're coming round, Axel!' replied my uncle. 'You call this splendid. We shall see finer things still, I hope. March! March!'

He might more appropriately have said 'Slide!' for we were just letting ourselves go without trouble on a comfortable slope—the *facilis descensus Averni* of Vergil. The compass pointed steadily to S.E.—the tunnel formed a straight line.

There was no great rise of temperature; this fact was in favour of Davy's hypothesis. I kept consulting the thermometer; two hours after the start it had only reached 10°, an increase of 4°.

About 8 p.m. my uncle gave the word to halt. Hans sat down at once, and we fastened our lamps to projections in the lava. We were in a sort of cavern in which air was not lacking—on the contrary, there were breezes, but I could not tell from whence. Hans spread out some provisions on a block of lava, and we all ate with appetite. One thing worried me rather: our water was about half finished, and we had so far seen no underground streams. I could not help drawing my uncle's attention to the subject.

'The absence of springs surprises you?' he said.

'Yes, and it makes me rather anxious; we have only enough water for five days!'

'Don't trouble, Axel; I'll answer for it that we shall find water, more than we want.'

'When shall we?'

'When we have got through this layer of lava. How could streams burst through these walls?'

'But perhaps the lava goes a long way down, and it seems to me we haven't gone very far vertically.'

'Why do you suppose that?'

'Because if we were at any depth in the earth, it would be much hotter.'

'According to *your* theory. Now what does the thermometer say?'

'Barely 15°, that is an increase of only 9° since we started.'

'Well, what do you conclude?'

'I believe that speaking generally the rise of temperature is 1° for every hundred feet down. But it varies, and in the neighbourhood of an extinct volcano may be 1° for 125 feet. Let us take this most favourable estimate, and calculate.'

'Calculate away, my boy.'

'Nothing is easier,' said I, putting down the figures in my note-book. '9 × 125 gives 1125 feet for the depth.'

'Your calculation is perfectly correct.'

'Well then?'

'Well then, according to my instruments, we have arrived at 10,000 feet below sea-level.'

The professor's observations could not be refuted; we were already 6000 feet below the mines, such as those in Tyrol and in Bohemia, and the temperature, which ought to have been 81°, was barely 15°. That was a subject for reflection.

NINETEEN

'WE MUST RATION OURSELVES'

Next day, Tuesday, 30th June, at 6 a.m. the descent was recommenced. We still followed the lava tunnel, a natural incline similar to those which take the place of stairs in some old houses. So it went on till 12.17, at which moment we came up with Hans, who had stopped.

'Ah!' cried my uncle, 'we have come to the end of the gallery.'

I looked round; we were at a fork, with two routes before us, both of them dark and narrow. Which ought we to take? That was a difficult question to decide.

My uncle, however, did not wish to show hesitation before either me or the guide; he pointed to the eastern tunnel, and soon we were all three engaged in threading it.

The slope of this new gallery was very slight, and its section very variable; sometimes a succession of arches appeared before us, like the aisles of a Gothic cathedral; the architects of the Middle Ages might have studied here the various forms of the pointed arch. A mile farther on, we would be bending our heads under low vaults of the Romanesque type, resting on thick pillars half-sunk into the walls.

The temperature continued quite bearable. I could not help thinking of what it must have been when the lava belched up by Snaefells rushed along this route, now so quiet! I imagined the fiery torrents breaking round the angles of the gallery, and the pressure of the superheated vapours in this narrow space!

'What *would* happen,' I thought, 'if the old thing were seized with an impulse of that kind now?'

I said nothing of this sort to Uncle Lidenbrock—he would not have understood. His one idea was to go on, walking, sliding, tumbling along even, with a conviction which one could not help admiring.

At 6 p.m., after a fairly easy day's work, we had gained six miles to the southward, but barely a quarter of a mile in depth. My uncle gave the signal to rest. We ate without many words, and slept without much reflection.

Our sleeping arrangements were very simple; we just rolled ourselves up, each in a travelling-rug. We had to fear neither cold nor interference. Travellers in the deserts of Africa or the forests of the New World are obliged to take their turns of watching during the night hours; but here there was absolute solitude and complete security—neither wild beasts nor savages to fear.

We awoke in the morning fresh and well, and resumed our journey, following a lava tunnel as before. But instead of plunging downwards into the earth, it was tending to become absolutely horizontal. It even seemed to me to be slightly rising. This became so marked by about 10 a.m., and consequently I grew so tired, that I was forced to go more slowly.

'What is it, Axel?' asked the professor impatiently.

'Well, I'm tired,' I answered.

'What, after three hours' walk on an easy path?'

'It may be easy, but it's certainly tiring.'

'What! when we've nothing to do but go down?'

'I beg your pardon, you mean go *up*!'

'Up!' said my uncle, shrugging his shoulders.

'Certainly. The slope began to change half an hour ago, and if we go on like this we shall certainly come to the surface of Iceland again.'

The professor shook his head with the air of a man who is not open to conviction. He answered nothing, and gave the signal to go on, and I saw that his silence was due to concentrated ill-temper.

I took up my burden again bravely, and rapidly followed Hans, who was now behind my uncle. I was most anxious not to lag behind and lose sight of my companions, shuddering at the thought of losing myself in the wanderings of this maze.

Besides, as the upward path became more and more fatiguing, I consoled myself with the thought that it would bring me back to the surface. This became a hope, confirmed at every step.

About noon the walls of the gallery changed their character. I noticed that they no longer reflected the light of our lamps so brightly. Instead of a coating of lava there were rocks disposed in sloping, often vertical beds. We were in the transition epoch, the Silurian period.

'It is evident,' I exclaimed, 'that these schists, limestones, and shales were laid down by water, and that we are turning our backs on the granite! We are like people of Hamburg who should take the Hanover road to reach Lübeck!'

I ought to have kept these remarks to myself, but my geological training got the better of my prudence, and my uncle heard my exclamations.

'What's the matter?' he said.

107

'Look!' I replied. 'We have come to the rocks of the period in which the first plants and animals appeared.'

'Oh, do you think so?'

'Look for yourself!' and I made him pass his lamp along the walls. However, he made no comment, but silently walked on. Either he did not like to confess that he had been mistaken in choosing the eastern tunnel, or he had made up his mind to explore it to the end. It was evident that we had quitted the route of the lava, and that we were not on the way to the source of that of Snaefells.

Still, I wondered whether I might not be mistaken, and decided to hunt for remains of primitive plants, which would corroborate my opinion.

Before I had gone a hundred yards I was rewarded by incontestable proofs—naturally, for in the Silurian epoch, the waters contained more than 1500 vegetable and animal species. My feet, which had grown accustomed to the hard lava, began to stir up a dust made of plant remains and shells. On the walls I distinctly saw the impressions of sea-weeds and lycopodiums; Professor Lidenbrock must have recognized them, but I believe he had his eyes shut—at any rate he marched on with an even step.

This was carrying obstinacy too far, and I could bear it no longer. I picked up a perfectly-preserved shell of an animal corresponding with our present-day wood-louse; then turning to my uncle I said, 'Look!'

'Well,' he said calmly, 'it's the shell of a crustacean of the extinct family of Trilobites, that's all.'

'But don't you infer——?'

'What *you* infer? Yes, I do. We have left the granite, and the lava streams. I may have been mistaken; but I shall know when we reach the end of this gallery.'

'That's right, Uncle; I should quite approve if we were not threatened with a constantly increasing danger.'

'And what is that?'

'The want of water.'

'Well, we must ration ourselves, Axel.'

TWENTY

A BLIND ALLEY

It certainly *was* necessary to ration ourselves. Our stock would not last more than three days, as I realized at supper-time. And unfortunately we had little hope of finding a spring in these Silurian beds.

The whole of the next day the gallery unrolled its interminable series of arches before our eyes. We marched on almost without a word, as if the taciturnity of Hans were catching.

The path did not rise, at any rate not noticeably; sometimes it even seemed to descend. But the beds remained the same, or rather gradually merged into those characteristics of Devonshire, which has given its name to the Old Red Sandstone. At times, too, the walls were clothed with magnificent specimens of marble, some of agate-grey with capricious white veins, some crimson, or yellow flaked with rose-colour, and farther on a variety spotted with dark-red and brown.

Most of these marbles showed traces of primitive animals; but since the period of the day before, creation had made distinct progress. Instead of the rudimentary trilobites, I saw the remains of more perfect creatures—amongst others, of Ganoid fishes, and of the Sauropteris, which palæontologists have considered to be the earliest form of reptile.

The Devonian seas were inhabited by a great number of creatures of this species, and they were deposited by thousands in the beds of the new period.

It was becoming evident that we were passing up the scale of animal life, which has man at the top; but Professor Lidenbrock appeared to take no notice, probably expecting either to come across a vertical shaft which would permit him to resume the descent, or to meet with an obstacle which would force us to return. However, the evening arrived without the realization of either expectation.

On the Friday, after a night in which I began to be distressed by thirst, our little band pressed forward again. After ten hours' marching, I observed that the reflection from the walls was greatly diminished. Marble, schist, limestone, sandstone were replaced by a dull, dark substance.

At a point where the tunnel was very narrow, I leaned against the wall; when I looked at my hand, it was quite black. I looked around more closely. We were surrounded by coal!

'A coal-mine!' I exclaimed.

'Without any miners,' replied my uncle.

'Ah! Who knows?'

'*I* know,' said my uncle shortly. 'I am sure that this gallery in the coal is not the work of man. But what does it matter? It's supper-time. Let us sup.'

Hans prepared some food. I ate little, and drank my meagre ration of water. Half of the guide's flask was all that was left for three.

After the meal, my two companions, rolled up in their rugs, found in sleep a respite from their fatigues. As for me, I could not sleep, and counted the hours till morning.

On Saturday at six we started again, and in twenty minutes

arrived at a vast cavern, evidently not hollowed by the hand of man, or the vaults would have been under-propped; it seemed as if only a miracle of equilibrium were keeping them up.

The cavern was about a hundred feet wide and perhaps a hundred and fifty high. The whole history of the Coal Measures was written on its walls, and a geologist could easily follow the successive phases. The beds of coal were separated by others of sandstone or of compact shale, and were greatly compressed by the weight of those above them.

At the period before that we call Secondary, the earth was subject to a tropical heat and incessant moisture; there were few trees; but immense grasses, ferns, lycopodiums, sigillarias, belonging to families which are rare now, but then contained thousands of species.

Now it is to this exuberant vegetation that the coal owes its origin. Subsidence took place, and the vegetable masses below the waters were first turned into peat, and then under the influence of fermentation were completely mineralized. Thus were formed the immense beds of coal which the consumption of all nations, for many centuries to come, will not exhaust.

I said to myself, however, that these particular beds would never be exploited—the labour required in reaching such remote sources would be excessive. Besides, why attempt it, when there is plenty of coal practically at the surface? Such as they were now, then, these beds would remain until the last trump.

However, we marched on, and I alone, probably, forgot the length of the way, wrapped up in geological considerations. The temperature remained almost constant, but my sense of smell informed me of the presence of carburetted hydrogen or marsh-gas, the explosion of which has led to such terrible catastrophes in coal-mines. How fortunate that we were lighted by Ruhmkorff's ingenious invention! If we had had the misfortune to explore this gallery by the aid of a torch, a terrible explosion would have ended the expedition by annihilating the explorers.

The march through the Coal Measures lasted till evening, my uncle growing more and more impatient at the horizontal nature of the track. I was beginning to think there would be no end, when suddenly, at 6 p.m., a wall appeared unexpectedly in front of us. Right, left, above, below, there was no opening. We had arrived at the end of a blind alley.

'Well, so much the better!' cried my uncle. 'I know where I am now. We are not on Saknussemm's road, and the only thing is to turn back. Let us take a night's rest, and before three days are over we shall be back at the place where the ways diverged.'

'Yes,' I said, 'if we have the strength!'

'And why not?'

'Because tomorrow the water will come to an end altogether.'

'And our courage too?' asked the professor, with a severe glance. I dared make no response.

TWENTY-ONE

THIRST!

Next day we started very early. Haste was important—we were five days' journey from the starting-point.

I will not weary you with the description of the sufferings of our retreat. My uncle met them with the anger of a man who is in the wrong; Hans with the resignation of a calm nature; for myself, I must confess that I complained and despaired, being unable to keep up my heart in such a misfortune.

As I had foreseen, the water gave out entirely at the end of our first day's march; henceforth we had nothing but gin, which infernal liquor burnt one's throat, so that I could not bear the sight of it. I found the heat suffocating, and was dropping with fatigue. More than once I actually almost sank unconscious; then my uncle and the Icelander stopped and did their best to comfort and strengthen me. But I noticed that the former was evidently feeling acutely the tortures of fatigue and thirst.

At last, on Tuesday, 7th July, crawling on our hands and knees, we arrived half dead at the junction of the two galleries. There I remained like an inanimate object, prone on the lava floor. It was ten in the morning.

Hans and my uncle, with their backs to the wall, tried to

nibble a little biscuit. Groans burst from my swollen lips. I fell into a deep stupor.

After a little time my uncle came to me and raised me up in his arms, saying, 'Poor child!' in a tone of genuine pity. I was touched by his words, not being accustomed to tenderness from the severe professor. I seized his trembling hands in mine, and he gazed at me with moist eyes.

Then he took the flask hanging at his side, and to my astonishment, held it to my lips, saying, 'Drink'.

Had I heard right? Was my uncle mad? I looked at him stupidly, incapable of understanding.

'Drink,' he repeated, and lifting the flask, he poured the contents into my mouth.

Oh, infinite joy! A mouthful of water slaked my burning thirst—only one mouthful, but it was enough to call back the life which was on the verge of departure. I thanked my uncle with clasped hands.

'Yes,' said he, 'a mouthful of water—the last, you know, the very last! I carefully kept it at the bottom of my flask resisting over and over again the terrible temptation to drink it! Well, you see, I kept it for you, Axel!'

'Dear Uncle!' I murmured, my eyes full of tears.

'Yes, you poor child, I knew that when you reached the cross-ways you would drop down half dead, so I kept these last drops of water to revive you.'

'Thanks, Uncle, thanks!' I cried.

Though my thirst could not be said to be in any degree slaked, I had recovered some strength. The muscles of my throat, which had been rigid, were loosened; my lips were less inflamed, and I could speak.

'Well,' I said, 'there's only one thing to be done now; we have no water, so we must go back.'

'Go back!' cried my uncle, but more as if speaking to himself than to me.

'Yes, and without losing a minute.'

'Then, Axel, that water has not restored to you your courage and energy!'

'Do you mean to say you won't go back?'

'Just when I see the possibility of success! Never!'

'Then we must be prepared to die?'

'You, Axel? No. Go back. I wouldn't be the cause of your death. Take Hans with you; I'll go on alone.'

'I couldn't leave you!'

'Yes, yes, leave me. I have begun this journey and I'll accomplish it, or never return. Go back, Axel, go back!'

My uncle spoke with extreme excitement. His voice, which had been tender, resumed its hard and threatening tone, as of one fighting with a gloomy energy against the impossible! I could not bear to abandon him in this abyss, though self-preservation counselled flight.

The guide followed this scene with his usual calm. He evidently understood from our gestures what the controversy was, but seemed little interested in a matter which concerned his very existence. I longed to have Hans on my side, but the difficulty was, how to communicate with him. I went up to him and laid my hand on his; he did not budge. I pointed upwards towards the crater, but he remained motionless, though my face and my panting breath betrayed my sufferings. At last he gently shook his head, and, quietly pointing to my uncle, said: 'Master.'

'Now, Axel,' said my uncle, 'listen to what I propose.'

I crossed my arms, and looked my uncle straight in the face.

'Our only difficulty,' he said, 'is the lack of water. In the eastern tunnel, made of schist, lava, and coal, we have found none. We may be more fortunate in the western branch.'

I shook my head in total incredulity.

'Hear me out,' said my uncle, raising his voice. 'While you were lying there motionless, I was observing the course of that shaft. It plunges straight downwards, and before long it will lead us to the granite core, where we should find abundant springs. Now Christopher Columbus asked his crews to have patience for three days; they agreed to this, though they were sick and terrified—and he discovered the New World. I am the Columbus of these subterranean regions, and I ask of you *one* day more. If, after that, we have not found the water we need, I swear to you to return to the surface.'

In spite of my irritation I was touched by these words, by the fact that my uncle was willing to make such a promise.

'Well,' I cried, 'let it be as you wish, and God repay your superhuman energy. You have only a few hours now in which to tempt Fate. Let us start!'

TWENTY-TWO

STILL NO WATER

The descent began again—this time by the new shaft. Hans went ahead, as he generally did. We had not gone a hundred paces, when the professor, passing his lamp along the walls, cried: 'This is the primitive rock! We are on the right track! Come on!'

Never had mineralogists found themselves so fortunately situated for studying nature on the spot. First there were schists, of beautiful shades of green, traversed by winding threads of bright metallic copper, manganese, or sometimes platinum or gold. To think of the riches thus buried in the bowels of the earth, for ever out of the grasp of human cupidity!

Then followed layers of gneiss, almost like those of sedimentary rocks, the beds being very regular and parallel; then the mica-schists disposed in thin flat flakes, the mica in them shining brilliantly. The beams of the lanterns, reflected by all the facets of the rocky mass, crossed and re-crossed each other in all directions, till one seemed to be progressing inside a hollow diamond.

Towards six in the evening this festival of light had noticeably diminished; the walls were duller, though still crystalline. Felspar and quartz appeared in conjunction with the mica, showing that we had reached the rock of rocks, the oldest and hardest, which sustains the weight of all the others. We were immured in an immense prison of granite.

It was now eight; still no water, and I was suffering anguish. My uncle was walking ahead, and would not stop, listening for the murmur of some stream—but in vain.

My limbs refused to support me; I resisted my tortures so as not to detain my uncle, but finally my strength failed completely—I uttered a cry of 'Help!' and fell down.

My uncle turned back. He gazed at me with his arms crossed, and muttered: 'That's the end!' He made an alarming gesture of anger, and then my eyes closed.

Some hours passed. I could not sleep, in spite of the profound silence, as of the grave. At last I thought I heard a slight sound, and then seemed to see the form of Hans disappearing into the darkness.

Why was he leaving us? I had the impulse to cry aloud, but then I was ashamed of my suspicions. It could be no flight—he was going *down* the gallery, not *up*. This thought allayed my fears, and then I began to consider why the quiet, passive Hans had risen from his slumbers. Was he on the track of some discovery. Had he, during the silence of night, heard murmurs which I had failed to catch?

TWENTY-THREE

——————◁○▷—————

'HANS IS RIGHT!'

For an hour my delirious imagination passed in review the possible motives of the taciturn guide. The most absurd ideas were jumbled together in my brain. I thought I was going mad.

But at last a sound of steps was heard in the depths below; Hans was coming up again. The uncertain light of his lantern began to shine on the walls, and then issued from the opening of the corridor. Hans appeared, went up to my uncle, laid his hand on his shoulder, and gently awakened him. My uncle got up.

'What is it?' he asked.

'Vatten,' replied the guide.

I guessed his meaning. 'Water! Water!' I cried, clapping my hands and gesticulating like a madman.

'Water!' repeated my uncle. 'Hvar?' he asked the Icelander.

'Nedat,' replied Hans.

Where? Down below! I understood. I seized the guide's hands and squeezed them, while he gazed at me quietly.

We made our preparations rapidly, and were soon descending a corridor with a slope of one in three. An hour later we had traversed about 6000 feet and so were 2000 feet lower.

At this point we distinctly heard a new sound, a sort of rumbling, like distant thunder, which seemed to be travelling behind the walls of granite.

'Hans was not mistaken,' said my uncle; 'what you hear is the noise of a torrent.'

'A torrent?' I cried.

'There is no doubt about it. There is a subterranean river near us.'

We hastened on, in the wild excitement of hope. I no longer felt fatigue—the sound of the water had already refreshed me. The torrent, which for some time had been over our heads, was now behind the left-hand wall, roaring and leaping. I kept passing my hand over the rock, hoping for traces of moisture, but in vain.

Half an hour passed, and we seemed to be *farther* from the stream, so we turned back. Hans stopped at the exact spot where it appeared to be nearest. I seated myself against the wall, and heard the water rushing with extreme violence about two feet away, but separated from me by the granite wall! I gave way to despair, but as Hans looked at me I thought I saw a smile on his lips.

He rose and took the lamp; I followed. He went up to the wall, placed his ear against it, and slowly moved from spot to spot with great attention. I understood that he was seeking the exact spot where the sound was loudest. He found it at three feet up from the path.

How excited I was! I hardly dared to guess what the guide proposed to do; but I did understand and applaud when I saw him raise his pickaxe to attack the rock.

'Saved!' I cried, 'saved!'

'Yes,' repeated my uncle in frenzied tones. 'Hans is right! Good fellow! We shouldn't have thought of that!'

He spoke truly; this simple method would not have entered our heads. And indeed it was certainly dangerous to attack with a pickaxe the scaffolding of the world. It might bring about some fearful crash which would overwhelm us! Or the torrent, bursting through the rock, might carry us away! These terrors were by no means groundless; but our situation was such that no fears of collapse or flooding could stop us, and our thirst was so intense that we would have dug into the very bed of the ocean to allay it.

Hans set himself to this work, which neither my uncle nor I could have tackled—we should simply have splintered the walls in our impatience. The guide, on the other hand, calm and moderate, wore away the rock gradually by repeated slight blows, producing a channel about six inches across. I heard the sound of the torrent increasing, and fancied I already felt the beneficent stream on my lips.

Soon the pickaxe had advanced two feet into the granite wall; the work had taken more than an hour, and I was writhing with impatience. My uncle wished to proceed to action himself; I could hardly prevent him—indeed he was seizing his pickaxe, when suddenly a hissing sound was heard. A jet of water leapt from the opening, and broke upon the opposite wall.

Hans, almost knocked down by the shock, could not repress a cry of pain. I understood why, when, plunging my hands into the jet, I in my turn exclaimed violently—for the water was boiling hot!

'Water at 100°!' I exclaimed.

'Well, it will cool down,' replied my uncle. The gallery was filling with vapour, and a stream was forming and running away along its subterranean windings; soon after, we were able to take our first mouthfuls.

Oh, what pleasure! what incomparable ecstasy! What was this water? Whence did it come? It matters little—it was water, and though still hot, it brought back the life which had been on the point of departing. I drank without stopping, without any sense of taste.

After about a minute's bliss, however, I exclaimed: 'It has iron in it!'

'Very good for us,' said my uncle. 'This journey is equivalent to going to Spa or Tœplitz.'

'Oh, how good it is!'

'I should think so; water from six miles down. It has an inky taste which is not unpleasant. And as Hans has procured it for us, I propose to give his name to the health-giving stream.'

'Good!' I cried. And the name of 'Hansbach' for the stream was at once adopted.

Hans gave himself no airs. After having refreshed himself moderately, he sat down in a corner with his usual calm.

'Now,' I said, 'we mustn't lose this water.'

'Why?' asked my uncle. 'I expect the source is inexhaustible.'

'Never mind, let's fill the barrel and the flasks, and then we'll try to stop up the opening.'

My advice was followed, With fragments of granite and tow, Hans attempted to stop the hole he had made. But he only succeeded in scalding his hands; the pressure was too great.

'After all,' said my uncle, 'why are we so anxious to stop this opening?'

'Why? Because——' and for the life of me I could not think of any very sufficient reason.

'When our flasks are empty, shall we be sure to be able to re-fill them?'

Of course we should not.

'Well then, let this water run on; it will naturally run downwards, and will guide us as well as slake our thirst.'

'That's a good idea!' I cried, 'and with this stream to help us, there is no reason why our plans should not succeed.'

'Ah, you're getting there, my boy,' said the professor, laughing.

'I've *got* there, in fact!'

'Wait a little, though. Let us begin by taking some hours' rest.'

I had really forgotten that it was night. The chronometer informed me of the fact, and soon each of us, restored and refreshed, was sleeping profoundly.

TWENTY-FOUR

---⊏○⊐---

UNDER THE OPEN SEA

Next day we had already forgotten our past troubles. At first I was astonished at not feeling thirsty, and wondered why it was. The murmuring stream running at my feet conveyed the answer.

We breakfasted, and drank of the excellent ferruginous water. I felt quite cheered, and prepared to go far; if it had been suggested to me to return to the summit of Snaefells I should have refused with indignation. But fortunately all we had to do was to go on downwards.

'Let us start!' I cried, awaking with my enthusiastic accents the ancient echoes of the globe.

The march was resumed on Thursday at 8 a.m. The winding granite corridor had all sorts of unexpected angles, but its general direction was consistently south-east. My uncle assiduously consulted his compass, noting the direction of our course.

This gallery was almost horizontal, with a slope of not more than two inches in six feet. The stream ran quietly; I thought of it as some familiar genius, guiding us through the labyrinths of earth, caressed its gentle warmth with my hand, and listened to the song which accompanied our steps.

As to my uncle, he was cursing the slightness of the slope,

and longing for a vertical shaft. But we had no choice, and if we were approaching the centre at all, however gradually, it was all to the good. Besides, every now and then the slope became greater; the stream tumbled down it, and we also descended more rapidly. Altogether, however, that day and the next we made considerable horizontal progress, but not much in the vertical direction.

On the night of Friday, 10th July, by our reckoning, we were ninety miles south-east of Reykjawik and at a depth of seven and a half miles. Then there opened beneath our feet an alarming-looking shaft, the steepness of which caused my uncle to clap his hands for joy.

'*Now* we shall get on,' he cried, 'and easily too, for the projections of the rock make a regular stair!'

The ropes were arranged by Hans in the safest possible way, and the descent began. I ought not to call it perilous, for I was now well accustomed to this method of progress.

The shaft was a narrow crack in the rocky mass, of the kind called a 'fault', produced by the contraction of the earth's crust as it cooled. There was no trace of any volcanic materials having passed through it. We were descending a sort of spiral stairway which might have been made by the hand of man.

At intervals of about a quarter of an hour we were obliged to pause for necessary rest, and to relieve the aching muscles of our legs. We would sit down on some prominent rock, with our legs dangling, talking while we ate, and drinking from the stream. Of course, in this fault, the Hansbach had become a waterfall, to the diminution of its volume; but it was still more than sufficient for us. Here it resembled my worthy uncle, with his impatience and fits of anger, while on the gentler slopes it was more like our Icelandic guide.

On the 11th and 12th of July we followed the spirals of this fault, penetrating six miles farther into the earth's crust, or about fifteen miles below sea-level. But on the 13th, the fault took a much gentler slope, leading south-east at an inclination of about 45°. The path became easy and monotonous—it could hardly be otherwise; one could not expect much enlivenment from the features of the landscape!

On Wednesday the 15th we were twenty-one miles underground, and about a hundred and fifty miles from Snaefells. Although a little tired, we were in good health, and our medicine-chest was untouched. My uncle made hourly observations of the chronometer, manometer, and compass (those which he has since published). When he told me that we had travelled a hundred and fifty miles horizontally, I exclaimed aloud.

'What is it?' he asked.

'If your calculations are correct, we are no longer under Iceland.'

'Do you think so?'

'We can easily see.' And with my compass, and the scale of the map, I took some measurements.

'I was right,' I said. 'We have passed Cape Portland, and those miles to the south-east have brought us under the sea.'

'Under the open sea,' repeated my uncle, rubbing his hands with pleasure.

'But think,' I said, 'the ocean is there over our heads!'

'That's nothing, Axel; at Newcastle there are coal-mines which extend under the sea.'

The idea made me rather uncomfortable however, though it could hardly matter whether the mountains of Iceland or the waves of the Atlantic were above us, so long as the intervening rocks held firm. But I soon became used to the idea, for the gallery, sometimes straight, sometimes winding, constantly varying its slope, but always trending to the south-east and descending, soon led us to great depths.

Three days later, Saturday the 18th, in the evening, we arrived at a sort of big grotto; my uncle gave Hans his weekly wages of three rixdollars, and it was decided that the next day should be one of rest.

TWENTY-FIVE

―――――◁[O]▷――――

A DAY OF REST

I awoke then on Sunday morning without the usual idea of having to prepare for an immediate start. And even in these depths, a holiday was still pleasant. Besides, we were accustomed to our troglodyte existence, and hardly thought of the sun, stars, and moon, trees, houses, and towns, of all those superfluities which our former life had taught us to regard as necessities. Living the life of fossils, we disregarded these unnecessary wonders.

The grotto formed a great hall, on the granite soil of which flowed the faithful stream. At this distance from its source, the water had only the temperature of its surroundings, and could be drunk without difficulty. After breakfast the professor occupied some hours in putting his daily notes into order.

'First,' he said, 'I shall make some calculations, to find out exactly where we are; and on my return I shall make a map of our journey, a sort of vertical section of the world with our course marked on it.'

'That will be very interesting, Uncle.'

'Now take the compass and see the direction in which we have just been travelling.'

I took it to the corridor, looked carefully, and replied: 'East-south-east'.

In the grotto

'Good!' said the professor, noting this and completing some rapid calculations. 'We have come 255 miles from our starting-point.'

'Then we are travelling under the Atlantic?'

'Exactly. And I estimate the depth at 48 miles.'

'But that is about the limit generally assigned to the crust of the earth!'

'I dare say it may be.'

'And here, according to the law of increasing temperature, we ought to be at 1500° C.!'

'*Ought* to be, my boy!'

'And all this granite ought to be melted!'

'Well, you see it isn't; what does the thermometer say?'

'27.6°.'

'So the scientists are just 1472.4° out! So that idea of constant increase is wrong. So Sir Humphry Davy was right, and I was right in believing him. What have you to say?'

'Nothing, except that I want to draw an inference.'

'Infer away, my boy.'

'At the latitude of Iceland, the radius of the earth is about 4749 miles, isn't it?'

'4750.'

'Call it 4800 in round numbers. And of that we have done 48, or one-hundredth?'

'As you say.'

'In twenty days?'

'Exactly.'

'Then it will take us 2000 days, or about 5½ years, to reach the centre!'

The professor said nothing.

'Besides which, if we go 250 miles horizontally for every

40 miles vertically, we shall come out somewhere long before we get to the centre!'

'Bother your calculations!' said my uncle angrily. 'The conditions may change. Besides, another man has done it, and if he has succeeded, so shall I.'

'I hope so; but after all, I may be permitted——'

'You may be permitted to hold your tongue, and not talk nonsense, Axel.'

I had the sense to be silent.

'Now,' he said, 'what does the manometer indicate?

'A considerable pressure.'

'Good. You see we have come to it gradually, and so feel no inconvenience.'

'No, except a little pain in the ears.'

'That will pass. Breathe deeply and quickly, to equalize the pressure in your lungs with that outside.'

'Yes, of course,' I said, determined not to annoy him. 'Have you noticed how clearly one hears sounds?'

'I have; it would make a deaf man hear.'

'But as the pressure increases, eventually the density of the air will be equal to that of water?'

'No doubt it will.'

'Then, how shall we get down then? We should float!'

'We shall put stones in our pockets.'

'Well, Uncle, you always seem to have an answer.'

The rest of the day passed in calculation and talk. I was always of Professor Lidenbrock's opinion, and envied the perfect indifference of Hans, who, without troubling about cause and effect, was prepared to follow blindly whither his fate led him.

TWENTY-SIX

I FIND MYSELF ALONE

It must be admitted that things had so far not gone badly on the whole, and I was beginning really to share my uncle's anticipations of glory.

For some days very steep slopes, some even so nearly vertical as to be alarming, took us deep into the internal mass; on certain of these we made a progress of four to six miles towards the centre. In these perilous descents, the skill of Hans and the marvellous way in which he kept his head were of the greatest use to us—indeed, we should never have come through some of them without him.

For another fortnight nothing took place worth recording, but then occurred an incident which I shall never forget, and with good reason.

On the 7th of August, our successive descents had taken us to a depth of ninety miles, and we were about six hundred miles from Iceland. That day the slope down was fairly gradual; my uncle had one of the Ruhmkorff lights, and I the other, and I was examining the nature of the granite. Suddenly, on turning round, I found myself alone.

'Well,' I thought, 'I must have walked too fast, or else my uncle and Hans have stopped somewhere. I must go back and find them. Fortunately it's not steep.'

I started back and walked for a quarter of an hour, looking about and seeing nobody, calling aloud and hearing nobody, my voice lost amid cavernous echoes. I began to feel nervous.

'I must be calm,' I said aloud to myself. 'I am sure to find them—there is only one path, and I was ahead. So I have only to go back.'

I did so for half an hour. I listened to hear if anyone was calling, and in that dense atmosphere sound carried marvellously. But an extraordinary silence reigned throughout the great corridor.

'Come,' I said to myself, 'it *must* be right to go back. The only thing is, when they lost sight of me, they might forget I was in front, and turn back themselves. Even then I should catch them up if I hurried. Of course!'

I repeated these last words to convince myself. Then a doubt seized me. Was I *sure* I was ahead? Yes, Hans was next, and then my uncle. I even remembered Hans pausing to adjust the burden on his shoulder, and my starting on again as he did so.

'Besides,' I thought, 'I have a sure guide in this labyrinth, a thread which cannot break, the faithful stream. I have only to follow it backwards, and I am sure to find my companions.

This thought cheered me and I blessed the forethought of my uncle, who had prevented Hans from stopping up the hole made for the issue of the water. I thought that before starting back again a wash in it would do me good, and I stooped to plunge my head in the Hansbach.

Judge of my horror when I found nothing but dry and sandy soil! There was no stream at my feet!

TWENTY-SEVEN

LOST!

I cannot depict my despair, for there is no word for it in any human language. I was buried alive, with the prospect of dying of the tortures of hunger and thirst. My burning hands felt the soil; how utterly dry it seemed!

But how had I left the course of the stream? For certainly it was no longer there! No doubt, at the moment when I had first started on this wrong path, I had failed to observe the absence of the stream. Evidently there had been a fork in the gallery, and I had taken one route, while the Hansbach, obeying the caprices of another slope, had led my companions into unknown depths!

How should I find them? My feet left no traces on the granite. I was lost, and I seemed to feel on my shoulders the whole weight of the ninety miles of rock above me! I was crushed.

At last, memories of my childhood brought with them the impulse to prayer, from which I rose in a calmer mood, and more ready to reflect on my situation intelligently. I had food for three days, and my flask was full; I must evidently go up and back, till I came to the fatal fork. There, with the stream to guide, I could regain the summit of Snaefells.

I rose, and leaning on my iron-shod staff, made my way

back, walking hopefully and unhesitatingly, knowing that there was no choice of routes. For half an hour there was no obstacle, and then I came to a place where there was no exit—solid rock in all directions!

I cannot describe my terror and despair. I was overwhelmed—my last hope crushed against that granite wall. Lost in a labyrinth which wound in every direction, I was doomed to the most terrible of deaths; and the whimsical thought came to me that if ever my fossilized remains were found ninety miles down, they would be the occasion of serious scientific controversy!

I tried to speak aloud, but only hoarse sounds passed between my dry lips, and I stood panting.

In the midst of this anguish, a new terror invaded my spirit. My lamp had been injured by a fall. I had no means of repairing it, and the light was failing and would soon be extinguished! I watched the light due to the electric current gradually fading in the filament of the lamp. A procession of shadows passed along the walls of the gallery. I would not lower my eyes for fear of losing the last of the fleeting illumination. Finally, only a feeble glow remained; I followed it with my eyes to the last, and when it vanished completely, and I was left in the profound darkness of the earth's interior, a terrible cry broke from me.

What is anything we call darkness on earth to this utter privation of all light? I was absolutely, hopelessly blind. I lost my head; sprang up, holding out my hands to feel; rushed haphazard through the winding corridors, calling, shrieking, howling, wounded by the sharp rocks, falling and rising again, bleeding, constantly expecting to dash my head against some obstacle and perish! At last I fell exhausted on the ground, and lost consciousness.

TWENTY-EIGHT

―――――◁o▷―――――

VOICES!

When I regained my senses, I found my face wet with tears. I cannot say how long my swoon had lasted—I had no means of knowing. Never had solitude been like mine!

I had lost much blood, and was covered with it. How I regretted not being yet dead, and that the ordeal was still to come! I felt about to faint again—this time probably without return—when a loud noise smote on my ears, like the prolonged rumbling of thunder.

Whence could the sound come? From some explosion of subterranean gas? I lay and listened for a repetition of it, but silence reigned, and I could no longer hear the beating of my own heart.

Suddenly my ear, applied to the rock as I lay, appeared to catch the sound of *words*—vague, indistinct, remote. I shivered, and thought, 'It is a hallucination!' But no—listening attentively, I did really hear a murmur of voices, though my brain was too feeble to grasp the meaning.

Dragging myself a few feet farther, I found I could hear more distinctly. I caught low murmured words, one of which was 'förlorad', spoken in a tone of distress.

Who was speaking? My uncle and Hans, evidently. But

if I could hear them, they could hear me. 'Help!' I cried with all my strength. 'Help!'

I listened tensely, but no answer could be heard. Perhaps my voice was too feeble. 'It must be they,' I thought. 'What other men are there ninety miles underground?'

I listened again. Placing my ear to the wall, I found the point at which the voices attained their maximum intensity. The word 'förlorad' came again to my ear, and the roll of thunder which had aroused me.

'No,' I said to myself, 'it is not through the rock that the voices reach me; they must come by way of the gallery itself—some peculiar acoustic effect.'

I listened again, and this time distinctly heard my own name, pronounced no doubt by my uncle, evidently talking with the guide, who had used the Danish word förlorad.

Then I understood. I must speak along the gallery, which would conduct the sound; but there was no time to lose—if they left that particular spot, the acoustic effect would be done away with. So standing alongside the wall I spoke as distinctly as possible—'Uncle Lidenbrock!'

I waited in extreme anxiety. Sound does not travel very fast, and increased density in the air does not augment its speed, but only its intensity. Some seconds passed, which seemed like centuries, before I heard, 'Axel, Axel, is it you?'

. . . .

'Yes, yes!' I replied.

. . . .

'My poor child, where are you?'

. . . .

'Lost in the deepest darkness!'

. . . .

'But your lamp?'

.   .   .   .

'Gone out.'

.   .   .   .

'And the stream?'

.   .   .   .

'Disappeared.'

.   .   .   .

'Axel, my poor dear boy, cheer up!'

.   .   .   .

'Wait a minute. I haven't the strength to talk—but talk to me.'

.   .   .   .

'Take courage, we have hunted for you vainly, and at last, supposing you still on the track of the stream, we have come down it, firing shots as signals. Now, though our voices can reach each other by some acoustic effect, our hands cannot touch. But don't despair, Axel.'

.   .   .   .

Meantime I was reflecting, and a ray of hope was returning to my heart. One thing was specially important. With my lips to the wall I said:
'Uncle!'

.   .   .   .

'Yes, my boy,' came back in a few seconds.

.   .   .   .

'We must know how far apart we are.'

.   .   .   .

'That is easy.'

.   .   .   .

'You have your chronometer? Take it, and say my name, noting the exact second. Instantly I hear the sound I will

140

repeat it, and you will again note the exact second at which the sound reaches your ear.'

.   .   .   .

'Right; and half the time will be that taken by sound in travelling the distance between us.'

.   .   .   .

'Now, begin.'

.   .   .   .

'Axel.'

.   .   .   .

'Axel,' I repeated as soon as I heard the word. Then I waited.

.   .   .   .

'Forty seconds,' said my uncle. So sound takes twenty seconds for the distance. At 1020 feet a second, that makes 20,400 feet, or a little under four miles.'

.   .   .   .

'Four miles!' I murmured.

.   .   .   .

'Well, that's quite a possible distance.'

.   .   .   .

'But should I go up or down?'

.   .   .   .

'Down—I'll tell you why. We are in a great big space, with a number of corridors leading to it. The one you are in is sure to bring you to us, for all these great cracks seem to radiate from this spot. So get up and walk, drag yourself if necessary, slide down the steeper slopes, and never fear that you will find us at the end. Start, my boy, start!'

.   .   .   .

'Good-bye for the present then, Uncle; I shall not be able to speak to you on the way.'

.   .   .   .

'No, but we shall meet.'

These were the last words I heard. After one prayer to God, whose mercy had led me to the only spot at which the foregoing conversation would have been possible, I started, revolving in my mind what I had heard of the Whispering Gallery at St. Paul's Cathedral in London, and especially of the Ear of Dionysus, the quarry at Syracuse in Sicily, where a whisper in one part is distinctly heard at one distant spot, and there only.

Judging by these instances, there could be no obstacle between myself and my uncle, and I had only to follow the path traversed by the sound to find him.

The descent was steep; I dragged myself or slid, and finally found myself travelling with alarming rapidity, which in my exhausted condition I was unable to moderate. Suddenly the ground failed under my feet; I found myself falling down a vertical shaft, hit my head on a sharp rock, and lost consciousness.

TWENTY-NINE

SAVED!

When I came to myself, I was in semi-darkness, lying on thick rugs. My uncle was watching my face for signs of life. At my first sigh he took my hand; when I opened my eyes he uttered a cry of joy.

'He's alive! He's alive!' he cried.

'Yes,' I answered feebly.

'My dear child, you are saved!' he exclaimed, straining me in his arms. It required an occasion like this to bring out his real tenderness.

Hans came up, looking distinctly pleased.

'God dag,' he said.

'Good day, Hans, good day,' I murmured. 'Now, Uncle, tell me where we are.'

'It's eleven o'clock at night; today is Sunday, 9th August, and you are not to ask any questions till the 10th.'

Certainly I was very weak; I dropped off to sleep at once, and slept profoundly.

Next day, on awakening, I looked round. My bed, made of travelling-rugs, was made up in a charming grotto, adorned with stalactites and floored with fine sand. It was only half dark, though no lamp nor torch was burning; but strange beams of light seemed to come from beyond, through a narrow opening into the grotto, and I also heard mysterious sounds like wind, and the breaking of waves.

I wondered whether I were really awake, or were still dreaming—perhaps the injury to my head caused me to imagine things. 'But no,' I thought, 'that really is light coming between the rocks, and I do hear the breaking of the waves, and the whistling of the wind! Are we back at the surface of the earth? Has my uncle given up the expedition, or completed it and returned?'

As I pondered these insoluble problems, the professor came in.

'Good morning, Axel,' he said joyfully. 'I am prepared to bet that you are feeling better!'

'I certainly am,' I answered, sitting up on the rugs.

'You ought to be, for you have slept well. Hans and I have watched you in turn, and he has anointed your wounds with some wonderful Icelandic remedy which has made them heal very quickly. He's a splendid fellow!'

As he spoke, my uncle was offering me food, which I devoured eagerly, in spite of his warnings as to caution. Meanwhile I overwhelmed him with questions which he hastened to answer.

It seemed that my providential fall had brought me just to the end of an almost perpendicular shaft; as I had come down in the midst of a torrent of stones, the smallest of which would have been sufficient to crush me, they concluded that a portion of the rock had slipped with me. This alarming vehicle had carried me, bleeding and swooning. right into the arms of my uncle.

'Now, for Heaven's sake, Axel, don't let us get separated again.'

Was the expedition not yet over, then? I opened my

eyes wide in astonishment, which provoked the question:

'What's the matter, Axel?'

'I want to ask you something. You say I'm all right, all my limbs—and my head?'

'Your head is all right except for some bruises.'

'But I'm afraid my brain is affected.'

'Why?'

'We have not come back to the earth's surface?'

'Certainly not.'

'Then I really must be mad, for I seem to see daylight, and hear the wind and the waves!'

'Oh! is *that* all?'

'Won't you explain?'

'I can't, for it's inexplicable; but you shall see, and you'll agree that geological science has still something to learn.'

'Let me go out and see!' I cried.

'No, Axel, no, the wind is very strong; you must have a little patience. A relapse would mean waste of time, which would be a pity, for the crossing may be rather a lengthy process.'

'The crossing?'

'Yes. Rest all today, and we will embark tomorrow.'

The word 'embark' excited me wildly. Was it a river, a lake, or a sea, and was there a boat moored on it?

My curiosity was so strong that my uncle saw that it would do more harm to check it than to indulge it, so he allowed me to dress. As an extra precaution I wrapped myself in one of the rugs, and then left the grotto.

THIRTY

THE SUBTERRANEAN SEA

At first I saw nothing. My eyes, unaccustomed to light, closed themselves involuntarily. When I opened them again, I was more astonished than delighted. 'The sea!' I cried.

'Yes,' said my uncle, 'the Lidenbrock Sea; it pleases me to think that no navigator is likely to dispute with me the honour of having discovered it, or the right of calling it by my name!'

A vast sheet of water, the beginning of a great lake or ocean, extended farther than the eye could see. The shore, with its great undulations, offered to the breaking waves a fine, golden sand, covered with the little shells characteristic of primitive types of creation. The waves broke with the peculiar sonorous murmur observed in great enclosed spaces; a light foam was carried by a moderate wind, and flecked my face occasionally. On this gently-sloping beach, at about six hundred feet back from the waves, came the feet of enormous rock-buttresses which then curved upwards to invisible heights. Some indeed came right down to the waves, forming capes and promontories, gnawed by the teeth of the surf. It was a true sea, with the capricious contour of our own shores, but deserted and horribly wild in aspect.

I was enabled to observe all these details by means of a peculiar kind of light. It was not the splendid irradiation of the sunbeams, nor the pale and vague rays of the moon. No—the penetrating nature of this light, its tremulous diffusion, its clear and dry whiteness, its coolness, its superiority in illuminating power to moonshine, evidently indicated a purely electric origin. It was like a permanent aurora borealis, filling the vast cavern which was capable of containing an ocean.

The vault above my head, the sky, if you like, seemed composed of great clouds, moving and changing masses of vapour, which, by condensation, must sometimes pour down in torrential rain. But just now it was 'fine weather'.. The effect of the light was intensely melancholy and sad. Instead of a sky shining with stars I sensed above those clouds a granite vault which overwhelmed my spirit by its weight, and however vast the space was, it would not suffice for the orbit of the least ambitious of the heavenly satellites.

We were indeed imprisoned in a vast hollow of the earth. We could not judge of its width, for it grew wider and wider as far as the eye could see; nor of its length, for our vision extended only to a somewhat indefinite horizon. As to its height, it must have been ten miles or more. The eye could not perceive the granite roof, but there were clouds which appeared to be at a height of at least two miles, higher than most clouds we are acquainted with, perhaps on account of the great density of the atmosphere.

I did not know what geological principles would explain the existence of this enormous excavation. Could the cooling of the earth have produced it? I was well acquainted, by reading, with some celebrated caverns, but their dimensions were nothing compared with these. The great Mammoth

Cave of Kentucky, for instance, is gigantic in its proportions, for its vault rises five hundred feet above an unfathomable lake, and travellers have gone more than thirty miles along it without coming to the end. But how could such a cavern be compared with the one I was now admiring, with its vault of cloud, its electric illumination, and a vast sea contained in its depths? My imagination failed before such immensity.

I contemplated these marvels in silence, unable to find words to express my sensations. I felt as if present at scenes in some far planet, Uranus or Neptune. New words were wanted for such new experiences, and I could not supply them. I looked, thought, admired with astonishment not unmingled with fear.

The unexpected nature of the scene had brought back the hue of health to my cheeks; I was being cured by wonder. Besides, the dense air was very revivifying, bringing a rich supply of oxygen to the lungs.

It may be conceived that after an imprisonment of over forty days in a narrow gallery, it was an infinite relief to breathe this wind, moist and saline; so I had no reason to repent having left the dark grotto. My uncle, already acquainted with these marvels, had ceased to wonder at them.

'Do you feel strong enough to walk about a little?' he asked me.

'Yes, certainly,' I said. 'I should like nothing better.'

'Well, take my arm, Axel, and we will follow the windings of the shore.'

I eagerly agreed, and we began to skirt this new ocean. On the left abrupt rocks, piled one upon the other, made a titanic heap. Down their flanks rolled innumerable cascades, clear and resounding; light spiral volumes of vapour coming from one rock or another indicated hot springs, and streams flowed peacefully towards the common receptacle, murmuring agreeably as they descended the slopes.

Among these I recognized our faithful companion, the Hansbach, which lost itself peacefully in the sea, just as if it had done so since the beginning of the world. 'We shall have to do without it for the future,' I said, with a sigh.

'Well,' said the professor, 'that stream or another, what does it matter?'

I thought the remark a little ungrateful!

However, at this moment my attention was attracted by an unexpected sight. On rounding a steep promontory we beheld before us, at a distance of about five hundred paces, a tall, dense forest. The trees were of medium height, of a regular parasol-shape, with sharp, geometrical outlines; the gusts of wind seemed to have no effect on their foliage, and they remained motionless like a group of petrified cedars.

I hastened to them, anxious to identify these extraordinary objects. Were they examples of any of the two hundred thousand plant-species so far discovered, or must they be accorded a special place amongst the flora of lakes? When we arrived under their shade, I recognized them for what they were—products of the earth, but conceived on a gigantic scale. My uncle immediately called them by their name.

'It's just a forest of mushrooms,' he said. He was not mistaken. It may be imagined to what an extent the circumstances would favour the development of a plant which loves warmth and moisture. Here were white mushrooms thirty to forty feet high, and with heads of an equal diameter. They were there in thousands; the light did not succeed in penetrating to the ground below them, and complete darkness reigned beneath these domes, crowded like the round roofs of an African city.

Yet I insisted on going farther. It was mortally cold under these fleshy vaults. For half an hour we wandered in these moist shades, and it was with a great sense of relief that I regained the sea-shore.

The vegetation of this subterranean country was not limited to mushrooms. Farther on there were groups of various other trees with pale foliage. They were easy to recognize as being some of our humbler plants grown to enormous dimensions, lycopodiums a hundred feet high, giant sigillarias, tree-ferns as tall as the pine trees of northern lands, lepidodendrons with cylindrical forked stems and branches, ending in long leaves and covered with coarse hairs.

'Astonishing, magnificent, splendid!' cried my uncle. 'Here we have the flora of the second period of the world, the epoch of transition. These are our humble plants which were trees in former times! Look, Axel, look! Never had a botanist such a feast for the eyes.'

'Right, Uncle. Providence seems to have preserved in this immense hot-house the antediluvian plants which scientists have so successfully reconstructed from their remains.'

'It certainly is a hot-house, my boy, and I think you might perhaps add, a menagerie.'

'How is that?'

'Look at this dust on which we are treading—these bones scattered on the ground.'

'Bones!' I cried. 'Yes, they are—bones of antediluvian animals!' And I flew upon these primeval relics, composed of the indestructible substance, calcium phosphate. Unhesitatingly I identified the gigantic bones, which resembled trunks of withered trees.

'This is the lower jaw-bone of a Mastodon,' said I; 'here are the molar teeth of the Dinotherium, and here is a femur which can only have belonged to the biggest of these monsters, the Megatherium. Yes, it is indeed a menagerie; for these bones have certainly not been transported hither; the animals they belonged to have lived on the shores of this sea, under the shade of these trees. Why, I even see whole skeletons. But——'

'But what?'

'But if antediluvian animals have lived in these subterranean regions, how do we know that they are not still wandering in these dark forests, or hiding behind these steep rocks?'

151

With this idea in mind I examined, with some alarm, the landscape in different directions; but no living creature appeared on the deserted shores. I was rather tired, so I went and sat on the end of a promontory at the foot of which waves broke noisily. From here I could see the whole bay, and in its curve, a little port between the pyramidal rocks, with calm waters sleeping sheltered from the wind, and capable of accommodating several yachts. I almost expected to see some craft issue from it under full sail and take advantage of the south wind.

This illusion, however, rapidly faded. We were indeed the only living creatures in this subterranean world. Whenever the wind sank, a silence deeper than that of the desert enveloped the arid rocks and hung over the surface of the ocean. Then I tried to penetrate the far-off mists, and to lift the curtain drawn across the mysterious horizon. What questions rose to my lips! How did this sea end? Whither did it lead? Should we ever see the opposite shores?

My uncle, on his part, had no doubts. As to me, I half desired the knowledge, and half feared it.

After passing an hour in the contemplation of this wonderful view, we returned by way of the shore to the grotto, and it was under the influence of the strangest thoughts that I fell asleep, and slept well.

THIRTY-ONE

THE RAFT

Next day I awoke completely cured. I thought a bath would be good for me, so I went to plunge for a few minutes into the waters of this Mediterranean Sea—as it certainly deserved to be called, better than its prototype above.

I came back with a good appetite for breakfast. Hans undertook the cooking for our little party; he had water and fire at his disposal, so that he could vary the meals to a certain extent. He served us with cups of coffee, and never did that delicious beverage seem more agreeable to the taste.

'Now,' said my uncle, 'the tide is rising, and we must not miss the opportunity of watching it.'

'The tide?'

'Certainly.'

'The influence of the moon and the sun is felt even here!'

'Why not? Are not all bodies subject throughout to the law of universal attraction? How should this mass of water be an exception to the general rule? Therefore in spite of the great atmospheric pressure on its surface, you will see it rise just as the Atlantic does.'

At this moment we were standing at the edge of the waves, and saw that they were gradually gaining on the shore. 'The tide is beginning to rise,' I said.

'Yes, Axel, and I judge that it will rise about ten feet.'

'How wonderful!'

'Not at all; it's natural.'

'You may say what you like, it *does* seem wonderful to me, and I can hardly believe my eyes. Who would have imagined that within the crust of the earth there was actually an ocean, with its ebb and flow, winds and storms!'

'Why not? Is there any law of nature to prevent it?'

'Not that I know of, if we abandon the idea of the central heat.'

'Then so far, Davy's theory is justified?'

'Certainly, and in that case there may be other seas and lands in the interior of the globe.'

'Yes—uninhabited, of course.'

'I don't know—why should there not be some unknown species of fish in these waters?'

'Well, we haven't seen a single one yet.'

'We can make some lines and hooks, and see if they will be as successful here as up above.'

'We will try, Axel, for we must penetrate all the secrets of these new regions.'

'But where are we, Uncle, by your instruments?'

'Horizontally, we are 1050 miles from Iceland.'

'As much as that?'

'I am certainly not more than a mile wrong.'

'And still going south-east, by the compass?'

'Yes. But with regard to the inclination, I have observed something very curious.'

'What?'

'That the needle instead of dipping towards the Pole, as it does in the northern hemisphere, on the contrary points upwards.'

'Does that mean that the magnetic pole is somewhere between the surface and the depth at which we have arrived?'

'Exactly, and no doubt if we were under the polar regions, near the seventieth parallel, where James Ross found the magnetic pole to lie, we should see the needle point vertically upwards. This mysterious centre of attraction is evidently not at a great depth.'

'Now, that is a fact which science has so far not suspected. How deep down are we?'

'One hundred and five miles.'

'So,' I said, examining my map, 'the mountainous part of Scotland is above us, and many miles overhead are the snow-covered summits of the Grampians.'

'Yes,' replied my uncle, laughing. 'There's a good weight to carry, but the construction is solid; the great architect of the universe has made use of good materials. What are the naves and arches of cathedrals compared with this vault, with a radius of nine or ten miles, and an ocean and its tempests amusing themselves under it?'

'Oh, I am not afraid of the roof falling in. Now, Uncle, what are your plans? Don't you mean to go back to the surface of the earth?'

'Go back indeed! On the contrary I mean to go on, as we have been so successful up till now.'

'Still, I can't see how we can penetrate below this liquid plain.'

'I don't mean to dive into it head first. But there can be no doubt that this internal sea is surrounded by a mass of rock.'

'Yes, of course it is.'

'Well then, on the opposite side I am sure to find some new way down.'

'How long do you suppose this sea is?'

'Perhaps ninety or a hundred miles.'

'Oh,' said I, thinking to myself that this estimate might be totally wrong.

'So there's no time to lose, and we must start off to-morrow.'

Involuntarily I looked round for the boat which was to carry us.

'I see,' I said. 'But what about a boat?'

'We have no boat, my boy, but we shall have a good solid raft.'

'A raft?' I cried. 'A raft is as impossible to construct as a boat, and I don't see——'

'You don't see, I dare say, Axel, but if you were to listen, you might hear!'

'Hear?'

'Yes, certain sounds of hammering which would show you that Hans is already at work.'

'Making the raft?'

'Yes.'

'What! Has he already felled the trees?'

'That was not necessary. Come and see him at his work.'

After walking for a quarter of an hour, on the other side of the promontory which formed the little natural port, I saw Hans at work; before long I was close to him. To my great surprise a half-finished raft already lay upon the sand, made of a particular kind of wood; and a number of beams, knees, and frames were scattered about—enough to construct a fleet of rafts!

'Uncle,' I cried, 'what wood is it?'

'It's pine, fir, birch, all sorts of northern trees, mineralized by the action of sea-water.'

'Really? Fossil wood? But then it must be hard like lignite, and too heavy to float?'

'That sometimes happens; but this is only partially fossilized. Look,' added my uncle, throwing one of the precious spars into the sea.

The piece of wood, after disappearing, rose again to the surface of the waves and floated about with their oscillations.

'Are you convinced?' asked my uncle.

'I'm convinced that it's incredible!'

The next evening, thanks to the skill of the guide, the raft was complete; it was ten feet long and five feet wide. The beams of fossilized wood, joined together by strong cords, formed a solid surface, and once launched, this improvised vessel floated peacefully on the waters of the Lidenbrock Sea.

THIRTY-TWO

———⊂⊂O⊃———

THE FIRST DAY'S SAIL

On the 13th of August we woke early. We were to start on a new form of locomotion, rapid and easy. A mast made of two staves spliced together, a yard made of a third, a sail borrowed from our store of rugs—such was our rigging. Ropes were not wanting, and the whole was taut and satisfactory.

At six o'clock the professor gave the word to embark. The provisions, baggage, instruments, arms, and a good supply of fresh water were placed on the raft. Hans had constructed a rudder which enabled him to guide the vessel. I loosened the cable which held us to the shore, the sail was set, and we started at once.

At the moment of leaving the little port, my uncle, who was interested in geographical nomenclature, suggested calling it after my name.

'If you ask me,' I said, 'I should like to give it another name. The name of Gräuben. Port Gräuben would look very well on the map.'

'Port Gräuben let it be.'

Thus the memory of my dear girl was associated with our successful expedition.

The wind blew from the north-east; we sailed before it

with extreme rapidity. The very dense air exercised a considerable force, and acted on the sail like a powerful fan. At the end of an hour, my uncle had made a calculation of our speed.

'If we go on like this,' he said, 'we shall travel at least ninety miles in the course of the day, and shall not be long in reaching the farther shore.'

I did not answer, but went to the fore part of the raft. Already the northern rocks were receding towards the horizon; the two shores to right and left were growing farther apart, as if to facilitate our passage. Before my eyes extended an immense sea; great clouds threw rapidly moving grey shadows, which seemed to cast an extra weight on the gloomy waters. The silver beams of the electric light, reflected here and there by spray, brought out luminous points on the sides of the raft. Soon all land was lost to view, no fixed object was visible, and but for our foaming wake, I could have believed that our craft was perfectly still.

Towards midday, masses of sea-weed appeared floating at the surface. I knew the wonderfully prolific nature of these plants, which grow at a depth of more than 12,000 feet at the bottom of the sea, under a pressure of four hundred atmospheres, and which often form masses considerable enough to impede the course of great ships; but never, I think, were sea-weeds as gigantic as those of the Lidenbrock Sea.

Our raft passed close to specimens of fucus three or four thousand feet long, immense serpents continuing beyond our view; it amused me to watch these infinite ribbons, always expecting to see the end of one, and for hours my patience was exercised without result.

Evening came on, but as I had observed the day before, the luminosity of the air was in no way diminished. It was a constant phenomenon, on which one could count. After supper I stretched myself at the foot of the mast, and was not long in falling asleep, to indulge in delightful dreams.

Hans, motionless at the tiller, let our vessel run before the wind; there was at present no need for steering.

From the time of our departure from Port Gräuben my uncle had kept a log-book, so that all I need do is to reproduce portions of it.

Friday, 14th August. Steady N.E. wind. Raft sailing fast and straight. Coast about ninety miles away. Nothing on the horizon. Intensity of the light does not vary. Fine weather, that is, the clouds are high up, not heavy, and flooded by a white, shining atmosphere like molten silver. Thermometer at 32° Centigrade.

At midday Hans fastened a hook on a line, baited it with a piece of meat, and let it down into the sea. For two hours he took nothing. Then a tug was felt; Hans drew in the line, and with it a vigorously struggling fish.

'A fish!' cried my uncle.

'It's a sturgeon,' I cried in my turn. 'A small sturgeon!'

The professor examined the creature carefully, and came to a different conclusion. The fish had a flat, rounded head, and the anterior part of its body covered by bony plates; its mouth was devoid of teeth, and its body was provided with fairly well developed pectoral fins, but had no tail. The creature certainly belonged to the family to which naturalists have assigned the sturgeon, but differed from the latter in essential details.

My uncle was not at a loss; after a short inspection, he said:

'This fish belongs to a family long since extinct, but found in a fossil state in the Devonian strata.'

'What!' I said, 'have we taken alive one of the inhabitants of those primitive seas?'

'Yes,' said my uncle, continuing his observations, 'and you see that these fossil forms are different from any present-day specimens. To find one of these creatures alive is a real treat to a naturalist.'

'But to what family does it belong?'

'To the order of Ganoids, family of Cephalaspides, genus——'

'Well?'

'Genus Pterychtis, I could swear; but this creature has a peculiarity which, they say, is met with among the fishes of subterranean waters.'

'What is that?'

'It's blind!'

'Blind!'

'Not only is it blind, but the organ of sight is entirely wanting.'

I looked—nothing could be more certain. But it may be a peculiar case, so the hook was baited and thrown out again. Certainly this ocean is very prolific, for in two hours we took a great quantity of Pterychtis, as well as fish belonging to another extinct family, the Dipterides, of a genus which my uncle could not identify; all were deprived of eyes. This unexpected haul was beneficial to our food-supply.

Perhaps, I thought, we may meet with some of the reptiles which science has succeeded in reconstructing on the evidence of a few remains of bone or cartilage.

I took the field-glass and examined the sea. It was deserted. Perhaps, I thought, we are still too near the shore. I looked upward. Why should not some of the birds reconstructed by the immortal Cuvier be exercising their wings in this heavy atmosphere? The fish would furnish them with sufficient food. No, the air and the shores seem to be equally uninhabited.

Now, however, my imagination carries me away amid the wondrous hypotheses of palæontology, and I indulge in a day-dream. I fancy I see at the surface of these waters the enormous Chersites, antediluvian tortoises like floating islands. On the sombre shores I seem to catch sight of the pachydermatous Lophiodon, an enormous kind of tapir, hiding behind the rocks, ready to dispute its prey with the Anoplotherium, a strange animal, related to the rhinoceros, horse, hippopotamus and camel. The giant Mastodon sways his trunk and breaks the rocks with his tusks, while the Megatherium, crouched on his enormous limbs, burrows in the earth, awaking the echoes with his bellowing. Higher up, the Protopithecus, the first monkey, climbs the arduous heights. Higher still, the Pterodactyl, with winged claws, flies like a great bat in the dense atmosphere. And above these again, immense birds, more powerful than the cassowary, larger than the ostrich, spread their wide wings and touch with their heads the very surface of the granite roof.

All this fossil world revives in my imagination, which goes back to the first days of Genesis, long before the birth of man, when the incomplete world was not ready for him. The centuries pass like days, as I pass backwards through the ages—the mammals disappear, then the birds, then the fish, crustaceans, molluscs. The zoophytes of the transition period pass into nothingness in their turn. The heat of the earth itself increases, and is greater than that received from the sun; the vegetation grows immense, and I pass like a ghost amongst tree-ferns, lean against the trunks of great conifers, or rest in the shade of lycopodiums a hundred feet high.

Then the plants themselves disappear; the granite rocks lose their solidity, the surface waters boil, and envelop the earth with vapour. Now the earth itself is a gaseous mass, white-hot, as large and as brilliant as the sun!

In the centre of this nebula I am carried through planetary space, my body is subtilized till I am an imponderable atom passing through infinite space in the vast orbit of the flaming globe!

I have forgotten the professor, the guide, and the raft in the intensity of my hallucination——

'What's the matter?' said my uncle. My wide-open eyes stared at him without comprehension.

'Take care, Axel, you'll fall into the sea!' At the same time I felt myself vigorously grasped by Hans. But for this, under the influence of my dream, I would have fallen into the waves.

'Are you ill, or mad?' cried the professor.

'No, I have had a hallucination, but it has passed away. Is all going well?'

'Yes, wind and sea are favourable.'

But there was still no sign of land on the horizon.

THIRTY-THREE

'WHAT IS IT?'

Saturday, 15*th August*. I notice that Professor Lidenbrock is like his old self, full of impatience. And yet, why be annoyed? Our voyage is proceeding amid favourable conditions—the raft is sailing with wonderful rapidity.

'You seem anxious, Uncle?' I said, seeing him constantly looking through his glass.

'Anxious? No.'

'Impatient, then?'

'One may very well be that!'

'But we are sailing fast——'

'What's the good of that? It's not that our speed is too small, but the sea is too big!'

I remembered then that the professor had estimated its length at about ninety miles. Well, we had travelled three times that distance, and still the southern shore was not visible.

'And we're not getting *down*!' resumed the professor. 'All this is waste of time—I didn't come all this way to go for a boating party on a pond!'

'But,' I said, 'as we've followed the course indicated by Saknussemm——'

'That's just what I'm not sure of. *Did* Saknussemm cross this water?'

'Anyhow, we can't regret coming here. This magnificent spectacle——'

'Don't talk to me of magnificent spectacles! I have an object, which I must attain!'

I stood corrected, and left the professor to bite his lips with impatience. Hans claimed his pay, and the three rix-dollars were counted out to him.

Sunday, 16th August. Truly this sea seems infinite! It must be equal to the Mediterranean, or perhaps the Atlantic—why not?

My uncle takes soundings by letting down a heavy pickaxe by a cord 1200 feet long. No bottom. We had difficulty in hauling in the weight. When it came up, Hans pointed out that the iron was marked as if it had been pinched between two hard bodies. I looked at him.

'Tander!' he said.

I did not understand, till the guide, by opening and closing his mouth several times, made his idea clear to me.

'Teeth!' I exclaimed in astonishment, considering the iron bar with greater attention. Yes, indeed, there were the marks of teeth on the metal. The jaws which contained them must have exercised prodigious force! Was it a monster of past ages, and was my dream of last night coming true? These thoughts kept me in excitement throughout the day, and I only calmed down at night.

Monday, 17th August. I am trying to remember the peculiarities of the creatures of the Jurassic period, when the earth seems to have belonged to the reptiles. How gigantic was their structure and how great their strength! The biggest and most terrible of the saurians of today, alligators and crocodiles, are greatly reduced copies of their ancestors of early times.

165

I have seen in the Hamburg museum the skeleton of one of these saurians, thirty feet long. Am I destined ever to find myself face to face with such a creature? Of course not—and yet—the marks of the teeth are on the pickaxe, and I can see that they were conical, like those of a crocodile!

I gaze in alarm at the sea, and my uncle seems to understand my thoughts, for he too, after having examined the pickaxe, keeps a sharp look-out on the ocean.

'Bother him!' I said to myself, 'with his notion of taking soundings. He must have disturbed some sea-creature in its retreat, and if we are not attacked on our raft——'

I cast an eye on our guns, to be sure they are in good condition and ready for use. My uncle makes a sign of approval.

Already great movements of the surface waters indicate some disturbance lower down. The danger is near. We must watch.

Tuesday, 18*th August*. Evening is coming on, or rather the time when sleep falls upon our eyelids, for there is no night on this ocean, and the implacable light fatigues the eyes, as in the Arctic summer we have left. Hans is at the tiller. During his watch I fall asleep.

Two hours afterwards, I am awakened by a violent shock. The raft has been lifted above the water with indescribable force, and shot a distance of a hundred feet or more.

'What is it?' cries my uncle. 'Are we aground?'

Hans points out, about a quarter of a mile away, a black mass alternately rising and falling. I look at it and exclaim:

'It's a colossal porpoise!'

'Yes,' replied my uncle, 'and now here is a sea-lizard of most unusual size.'

'And farther off a monstrous crocodile! Look at its great jaws and rows of teeth! Oh, it's disappearing!'

'A whale! A whale!' then cried the professor. 'See the air and water it is blowing up!'

And indeed, two liquid columns are driven to a great height above the sea. We are surprised, stupefied, terrified by this flock of sea-monsters of supernatural dimensions, the smallest of whom could break our raft with his teeth. It is impossible to flee—we are surrounded, and I take my rifle, well knowing, however, that a bullet is likely to make little impression on these scaly hides.

We are mute with fear; they are approaching—on one side the crocodile, on the other a serpent, thirty feet long, darting its enormous head to and fro above the waves. All the other creatures have disappeared. I am about to fire, when Hans stops me by a gesture. The two monsters pass the raft at a distance of about three hundred feet, flinging themselves on each other, and disregarding us entirely in their fury.

The fight begins about five hundred feet away; we can distinctly see the two struggling monsters. But now it seems to me that the other animals are coming to take part in the strife, the porpoise, whale, lizard, tortoise—I catch glimpses of them every now and then. I show them to the Icelander, but he shakes his head.

'Tva,' he says.

'What, *two*? He declares that there are only two animals——'

'He's right,' cries my uncle, his glass at his eyes. 'The first of these monsters has the snout of a porpoise, the head of a lizard, the teeth of a crocodile; that is what put us out. It is the most formidable of the antediluvian reptiles, the Ichthyosaurus!'

'And the other?'

The battle

'The other is a serpent rising from the shell of a tortoise, the deadly enemy of the first, the Plesiosaurus!'

Hans is right. Two monsters only are thus troubling the surface of the sea, and I have before my eyes two reptiles of the primitive oceans. I see the bloodshot eye of the Ichthyosaurus, as big as a man's head. Nature has endowed it with an extremely powerful optical apparatus, capable of withstanding the pressure of the water in the depths at which it lives. It has been rightly called the saurian whale, for it has the speed and somewhat the form of a whale. It measures not less than a hundred feet, and I can judge of its size when it lifts above the waves the vertical tail-fins. The jaw is immense, and the naturalists say it contains not less than 182 teeth.

The Plesiosaurus, a serpent with a cylindrical body, and a short tail, has its limbs in the form of oars. Its body is entirely covered by a scaly carapace, and its neck, as flexible as a swan's, rises thirty feet above the water.

These animals attack each other with an indescribable fury. They raise mountainous waves which reach as far as the raft, so that twenty times we are at the point of being swamped. Hissing sounds of prodigious intensity are heard. The beasts are intertwined, and can no longer be distinguished apart, and there is everything to be feared from the fury of the conqueror!

An hour, two hours elapse, and the fight goes on with the same energy, the combatants alternately nearing the raft and going farther away. We remain motionless, prepared to fire.

Suddenly both creatures disappear, causing a veritable whirlpool. Will the fight end in the depths of the sea? But now an enormous head shoots upwards, that of the Plesiosaurus. The monster has had his death-wound; I can no longer see the great shell, but his long neck rises, falls, curves, and circles, striking the waves like a great lash, and twisting like a wounded worm. The water splashes afar, and blinds us. But soon the death-agony is nearly over, the movements diminish, the contortions cease, and the long serpent form lies an inert mass on the calmed waves.

As to the Ichthyosaurus, has he regained his submarine cavern, or will he re-appear at the surface of the sea?

THIRTY-FOUR

AXEL ISLAND

Wednesday, 19*th August*. Fortunately the strong wind has enabled us to get away quickly from the battlefield. Hans is still at the tiller, and my uncle, after the distraction of the fight, has fallen back into his impatient watching of the sea.

Thursday, 20*th August*. Wind N.N.E., variable. Temperature high. Our speed is about ten miles an hour. Towards mid-day a very distant sound is heard—an incessant low roar which I cannot explain.

'Some rock or island,' says the professor, 'with the waves breaking against it.'

Hans climbs to the top of the mast, but can see no rock. The ocean is uniform to the horizon-line. Three hours go by; the sound seems that of a distant waterfall, and so I remark to my uncle, but he shakes his head. All the same I feel sure I am right, and wonder whether we are not running straight into some cataract which will carry us into an abyss. I dare say my uncle would be glad, with his love of the vertical, but for my part——

Anyhow, there must be a good way to leeward some very noisy phenomenon, for now the roaring sound has become very distinctly audible. Does it come from the sky or the sea? I look upwards to the clouds and try to penetrate their

171

depths. The sky is tranquil; the clouds, high up in the vault, seem motionless, and lose their outline in the intense luminous irradiation. The explanation must evidently be sought elsewhere.

Then I gaze at the horizon, which is clear and free from mist. No change in its aspect. But if the noise comes from a waterfall—if all this sea is emptying itself into a lower basin, if these rumblings are produced by the mass of falling water, there should be a current to indicate this, and its increasing speed will give warning of the peril before us. I therefore throw out an empty bottle; but there seems to be no current—it is simply driven by the wind.

About four o'clock Hans gets up and climbs the mast again. Thence his glance circles round the horizon and stops at a certain point. He shows no surprise, but his gaze is fixed.

'He has seen something,' says my uncle.

'Yes, I think he has.'

Hans comes down, then pointing southwards he says: 'Der nere!'

'Down there?' repeats my uncle. And seizing his field-glass, he gazes attentively for a minute, which seems a century to me.

'Yes, yes,' he cries.

'What can you see?'

'An immense jet rising above the waves.'

'Another sea-beast?'

'Perhaps.'

'Then let us steer more to westwards, for we have had quite enough experience of these antediluvian monsters!'

'No, straight on,' replies my uncle.

I turn to Hans, but he holds his rudder with inflexible determination.

And yet, if we can see, at a distance of at least thirty miles, as it must be, the column of water thrown up by this animal, it must be of a supernatural size. The most ordinary prudence would counsel flight; but we have not come here to be prudent. So we go on, and the apparent size of the jet constantly increases. What monster can take in such a quantity of water and expel it without interruption?

At eight o'clock in the evening we are about five miles away from it. The dark, enormous, monstrous body extends in the sea like an island. Is it illusion or fear—it seems to me more than a mile long! It is motionless and seems asleep, not heaving on the sea, but sending up a column of water five hundred feet high. My terror is such that I prepare to cut the halyard, for I *will* not drift straight upon it!

Suddenly Hans rises, and pointing forward says: 'Holm.'

'An island!' cries my uncle, with a great shout of laughter.

'But that jet of water?'

'Geysir,' says Hans.

'Ah, no doubt, a geyser,' replies my uncle, 'a geyser like those in Iceland.'

As we approach, the truth of this explanation becomes evident, though the island has a remarkable resemblance to an enormous whale with a head about sixty feet above the waves. The geyser (an Icelandic term meaning 'fury') is of magnificent dimensions, and rises near one end of the island. Loud explosions are heard at certain moments, and the enormous jet, seized with more violent rage, shakes its vaporous plume and shoots up to the lower clouds. It is the only one; there are neither fumaroles nor hot springs in the neighbourhood, and all the volcanic force is concentrated in the geyser.

'Let us come alongside,' says my uncle.

But we are obliged to be very careful in avoiding the flow of water, which would swamp the raft immediately. Hans, however, manages to bring us skilfully to the end of the island.

I spring ashore, quickly followed by my uncle, while Hans remains at his post, apparently superior to curiosity.

We walk on granite mingled with siliceous tufa; the ground trembles under our feet like the sides of a caldron full of superheated vapour—it is burning hot. We come in sight of a little central basin from which the geyser rises, and I plunge a thermometer into the water, which is boiling as it runs; 163° C.!

It seems to me that though we have been remarkably favoured as to temperature so far, we shall undoubtedly arrive before long at those regions where the central heat passes all ordinary limits.

'We shall see,' is all the professor will say; and after naming the volcanic island after his nephew he gives the signal to re-embark. I continue to watch the geyser, and notice that its volume varies, suddenly increasing and diminishing, a fact which I attribute to variations in the pressure of the vapours accumulated below.

Then we set sail again, coasting along by the upright rocks of the southern end. Hans has put the raft in good condition during our absence. I note that we have sailed 810 miles from Port Gräuben, and we are 1860 miles from Iceland, beneath England.

THIRTY-FIVE

THE STORM

Friday, 21*st August*. Today the magnificent geyser has disappeared. The wind has freshened, and carried us fast away from Axel Island, and the rumblings have gradually become inaudible.

The weather, if I may so call it, seems about to change. The atmosphere is filling with vapours charged with electricity, the clouds are lower, and of an olive hue; the electric light can hardly pierce the curtain of the theatre where the storm-drama is apparently to be played.

I am affected as one often is at the coming of a storm. The heaped-up cumulus clouds in the south have a sinister and pitiless look. The air is heavy; the sea is calm.

Far off the clouds resemble great bales of cotton; gradually they swell, becoming fewer and bigger. They seem too heavy to rise; in the end they mingle together, forming one great menacing mass.

Evidently the atmosphere is full of electricity; I am the same myself—my hair stands out as from the effects of an electric machine. I feel as if my companions would receive a shock if they touched me. By ten in the morning the signs are still more decisive; one would say the wind was softening just to take breath, and the bank of cloud looked like a great cave in which storms were brooding.

I try to think nothing of these threats, and yet I can't help saying:

'It looks like bad weather.'

The professor makes no answer. He is intensely vexed at seeing the ocean extending indefinitely before us. He only shrugs his shoulders. There is a general silence. The wind fails—Nature seems dead, having ceased to breathe. The sail droops along the mast, and the raft is motionless on the heavy, waveless sea. But in that case, why keep up this sail, when it may prove our destruction at the first onset of the storm?

'Let us lower it,' I say, 'and take down the mast; that is the prudent course.'

'No, no, in the devil's name!' cries my uncle. 'Let the wind and the storm seize us and carry us away; if only they will bring us to shore, I don't mind if our raft is broken in pieces against it!'

Almost before the words are out of his mouth there is a sudden change on the southern horizon; the accumulated vapours are condensed into water, and the wind, rushing from the farthest extremities of the cavern, blows with tempestuous violence; while the darkness increases till I can hardly take the roughest notes.

The raft is lifted, and leaps forward. My uncle is flung down, and I crawl to him. He is holding tightly to a cable, and seems to enjoy the scene. Hans is motionless. His long hair emits sparks from the extremities, and his strange face suggests that of an antediluvian.

The mast holds good, though the sail swells like a bubble on the point of bursting; the rain forms a roaring cataract,

176

veiling the horizon towards which we are wildly fleeing. But before we reach this veil it is torn asunder by electric forces; peals of thunder are mingled with brilliant flashes of lightning. The vaporous mass becomes incandescent, and the hailstones striking the metal of our tools or guns are rendered luminous; the heaving waves are fire-crested.

My eyes are dazzled by the intensity of the light, my ears deafened by the crash of the thunder; I am obliged to cling to the mast, which is bending like a reed.

.　　.　　.　　.　　.　　.　　.　　.

(Here my notes become very incomplete. I have only discovered a few more fugitive observations. Still, perhaps their very brevity and incoherence gives a sense of the emotions which dominated me.)

.　　.　　.　　.　　.　　.　　.　　.

Sunday, 23rd August. We have been carried with unheard of rapidity—where are we? The night has been awful; no calm yet—incessant explosive noise. Our ears are bleeding, and we cannot exchange a word.

The lightning goes on and on. I see zigzags coming down and then up again to the granite roof. If it should fall in! Then there are globes of fire which burst like bombs, but without increasing the noise, for it is already as great as the human ear can distinguish.

Monday, 24th August. Will it never end? We are overcome with fatigue, all but Hans. We still run to the south-east, and have travelled more than 600 miles from Axel Island.

At midday the violence of the storm is still greater; we lash everything to the raft, including ourselves, and let the waves pass over our heads. It has been impossible to speak all the time, but I write down: 'Let us get rid of the sail,' and my uncle makes a sign of assent.

But suddenly a fiery ball appears near the raft, and at the same moment the mast and sail are carried away and lifted to a prodigious height, where they take on the appearance of the Pterodactyl, the fantastic bird of early ages.

We are paralysed with fear; the fireball, half white, half blue, about ten inches across, moves about slowly, but rotates with extreme rapidity under the lash of the storm. It saunters here and there, perches on one of the planks of the

raft, springs on the bag of provisions, leaps lightly down, rebounds and touches the powder-canister. Horrors! it will explode! No, the bright thing moves off—hovers about Hans, who simply gazes at it—about my uncle, about myself. It spins round near my foot, which I try to remove, but find it impossible. A smell of nitrous gas fills the atmosphere, filling our lungs to suffocation.

Why cannot I withdraw my foot? Ah, I see, the electric globe has magnetized all the iron; the instruments, tools and guns are moving and clinking, and the nails in my boot are strongly adhering to an iron plate fastened to the wood.

In the end, with a violent effort, I drag my foot away just as the fire-ball seemed about to seize it——

Ah, what an intense light! The globe has burst into a myriad of flaming jets! Now all is over. I have just seen my uncle stretched on the raft, and Hans still at the rudder, but 'spitting fire' under the influence of the electricity with which he is saturated.

Where are we going? Where are we going?

．　　．　　．　　．　　．　　．　　．

Tuesday, 25*th August*. I am coming out of a long swoon; the storm goes on—the lightning-flashes are like serpents.

A new sound is heard—breakers against rocks! But then

．　　．　　．　　．　　．　　．　　．　　．

THIRTY-SIX

WHERE ARE WE GOING?

Here ends what I have called 'my log', fortunately saved from shipwreck. I return to my ordinary narrative.

What happened when we struck the rocks, I cannot say. I felt myself flung out, but was preserved from injury by the strong arm of Hans. The brave Icelander carried me to a hot, sandy beach, where I lay alongside of my uncle, while he went back to see what he could save from the wreck.

The rain continued to pour; we found shelter under some rocks, and Hans prepared some food which I was unable to touch; then we all slept the sleep of exhaustion.

Next day it was beautifully fine. All traces of the storm had vanished when I was awakened by my uncle's joyful tones:

'Well, my boy, have you slept well?'

'Very well,' I answered. 'I feel knocked about, but that will pass. You seem very cheerful this morning, Uncle!'

'Delighted, my boy, delighted! We have arrived!'

'At the end of our expedition?'

'No, but at the end of this sea, which appeared interminable. Now we shall be able to get down into the earth again.'

'Uncle, may I ask one question?'

'You may, Axel.'

'Well, what about the return journey?'

'The return! So you're thinking of getting back before we've got *there*!'

'I only wanted to know how we are going to manage it.'

'That's very simple. When we are at the centre of the earth, we shall either find some new route to the surface, or we shall pursue the uninteresting course of returning by the way we came. I have no reason to suppose it will close up behind us.'

'Then we must repair the raft.'

'Certainly.'

'But shall we have enough provisions?'

'Yes, indeed. Hans is an able fellow, and I am sure he will have saved most of our cargo. Let us go and see.'

We quitted the grotto and went to the shore, where we found Hans in the midst of a number of neatly arranged objects. My uncle squeezed his hand with intense gratitude; for this man, with unexampled devotion, had worked while we slept, and saved all the most precious things at the risk of his life.

Not that we had not some serious losses, for instance our guns—but after all we could manage. The powder was still intact.

'Well,' said the professor, 'we shall not be able to go out shooting, that's all.'

'And what about the instruments?'

'Here is the manometer, the most useful of all, for by it I can calculate the depth, and know when we reach the centre! Otherwise we might go too far and come out at the Antipodes!' His gaiety was really ferocious.

'But the compass?' I asked.

'Here it is, on this rock, in perfect condition, and so are the chronometer and the thermometers. Hans is a wonderful man!'

The instruments were indeed all there, and many of the tools were lying on the sand, ladders, ropes, pickaxes, etc.

'What about provisions?' I said.

'Let us see,' answered my uncle.

The cases which contained them were arranged in rows on the shore, and were in a perfect state of preservation; what with biscuits, salt meat, dried fish, and gin, we could count on food for four months yet.

'Four months!' cried the professor; 'we have time to get there and back, and with what is over I will give a great dinner to my colleagues at the Johannæum!'

I ought to have known my uncle by now, but somehow he still astonished me.

'Let us breakfast,' he said now. I followed him to a raised promontory, after he had given instructions to the guide. Dried meat, biscuits, and tea were the ingredients of one of the most excellent meals I have ever eaten. Hunger, the fresh air, tranquillity after agitation, all contributed to give me an appetite.

During breakfast I discussed with my uncle the question of where we were.

'It seems to be very difficult to calculate,' I said.

'Yes, to calculate exactly—in fact impossible,' he replied; 'for during these three days of storm I have been unable to note the speed and the direction of the raft's course; but we can estimate it approximately.'

'Well, the last observations were made at the island with the geyser——'

'At Axel Island, my boy. Do not refuse the honour of

giving your name to the first island discovered in the interior of the earth.'

'Very well, at Axel Island we had traversed about 810 miles of this sea, and were more than 1800 miles from Iceland.'

'Good—let us start from that, and count four days of storm, during which we can hardly have done less than 240 miles in the 24 hours.'

'I agree. So that will be 900 to 1000 miles to be added.'

'Yes and the Lidenbrock Sea would be about 1800 miles from shore to shore! Do you know, Axel, that it would compete with the Mediterranean in size?'

'Yes, especially if we have only traversed the *width* of it!'

'Which is quite possible.'

'And another curious thing is that if our calculations are correct, we have the Mediterranean now over our heads. We are about 2700 miles from Reykjawik.'

'That's a good distance, my boy; but as to whether we are under the Mediterranean, and not rather under Turkey or the Atlantic, we can only reckon on the supposition that our direction has been constant.'

'The wind certainly seemed constant; so I believe this shore is south-east of Port Gräuben.'

'Well, we can easily make sure by consulting the compass.'

The professor approached the rock on which Hans had laid the instruments. He was gay and cheerful, rubbing his hands and attitudinizing like a youth! I followed him, rather curious to know how near my estimate was.

Arriving at the rock, my uncle took the compass, placed it level and observed the needle, which after some oscillations took up the position due to the influence of magnetic force.

He gazed at it, rubbed his eyes and gazed again. At last he turned to me, bewildered.

'What's the matter?' I asked. He signed to me to look for myself. An exclamation of surprise escaped me; for the north-pointing end of the needle turned straight towards the land instead of to sea—the exact opposite of what we expected!

I shook the compass, but in vain. So the wind must have changed without our noticing it, and we were back on the shore from which we had started!

THIRTY-SEVEN

A HUMAN SKULL!

It would be impossible to describe the succession of emotions which agitated Professor Lidenbrock—astonishment, incredulity, and finally anger. I never saw a man at first so taken aback, and then so irritated. The fatigues of the crossing, the dangers encountered—were all these to be experienced over again? Had we gone backward rather than forward?

However, my uncle soon became master of himself.

'So these are the tricks fortune plays on me!' he cried; 'the elements conspire against me; air, fire, and water combine to block my way! Well, they shall know the strength of my will. I will not yield a pace, and we shall see which will win, man or nature!'

Standing on the rock, irritated and menacing, Otto Lidenbrock, like Ajax, seemed to be defying the gods. But I thought it well to intervene and put some check on this wild energy.

'Listen to me,' I said firmly. 'There is a limit to ambition in this world; we are ill-equipped for a sea-voyage, for fifteen hundred miles are not to be accomplished on a poor collection of planks, with a rug for sail, a staff for mast, and against the wind. We cannot steer, we are at the mercy of the storms, and it is the part of madmen to attempt this out-rageous crossing a second time!'

For ten minutes I was allowed to pour forth such irrefut-able arguments, simply because the professor was paying not the smallest attention to them.

'To the raft!' he cried. This was his only answer, and in vain I reasoned, prayed, and grew angry; I had to do with a determination stronger than granite.

Hans had just finished repairing the raft with some new pieces of fossilized wood. The new sail was already rising, and the wind playing in its folds. The strange man seemed to understand my uncle's intentions.

The professor said a few words to him, and he immediately loaded the raft with our effects and made all ready for starting. The weather was clear and the wind from the north-west. What could I do? I could not oppose the two, and Hans appeared to be absolutely at his master's bidding, so I was preparing to take my place on the raft, when my uncle's hand held me back.

'We won't leave till tomorrow,' he said.

I made a gesture of complete resignation.

'I must neglect nothing,' he said, 'and as fate has driven me on this part of the coast, I will not leave it without having explored it.'

This remark will be understood when it is explained that if we had returned to the north shore, it was not the place from which we had started. Port Gräuben must, we con-sidered, be more to the west. It was therefore a sensible idea to examine thoroughly our new surroundings.

'Let us explore!' I said.

The space between the waves and the foot of the cliffs was here very broad; one might walk for half an hour before reaching the latter. Our boots crushed innumerable shells of all shapes and sizes, the remains of prehistoric creatures. I also saw enormous carapaces, sometimes fifteen feet across, which had belonged to beasts of which the modern tortoise is but a greatly reduced reproduction. Besides this, the stones covering the ground were rounded, and disposed in rows and layers; from all of which I concluded that at one time the sea had covered this part, now beyond its range.

To explain the existence of this ocean, 120 miles below the surface of the earth, I supposed that there had been a fissure through which the waters had penetrated from above, but that it had been subsequently filled up, otherwise this whole vast cavern would have become full of water. Perhaps, too, this water, in contact with subterranean heat, had evaporated to a great extent; this would account for the clouds over our heads, and the electric storm which we had experienced.

I felt satisfied when I had evolved this theory of the phenomena of which we had been witnesses; however great are the wonders of nature, there is always an explanation, according to the laws of physics.

We had followed the shore for about a mile, when the appearance of the rocks suddenly changed. They appeared to have been displaced by some violent upheaval of the lower strata, and in many parts there was evidence of dislocation.

We advanced with difficulty over granite boulders, mingled with flint, quartz, and alluvial deposits, and suddenly came in sight of a field, or rather a plain, full of bones. It gave the impression of an immense cemetery, containing the remains of twenty centuries of mortality, and extending to the horizon, where it was lost in the mist.

We were drawn forward by burning curiosity. Our feet trod with a crackling sound on vestiges of prehistoric beasts, the rare and interesting relics of which are eagerly competed for by our museums. A thousand Cuviers would have been needed to reconstruct all the skeletons in that vast ossuary.

I was stupefied. My uncle lifted his long arms towards the vault which served for sky. His mouth was wide open, his eyes blazed behind his glasses, his head swayed up and down, right and left—his whole expression denoted the extreme of astonishment. He was confronted with a priceless collection, including the Leptotherium, the Mericotherium, the Mastodon, the Protopithecus, the Pterodactyl, all heaped up there for his personal satisfaction. Imagine a passionate bibliomaniac suddenly transported into the famous library of Alexandria which Omar burned and which we suppose miraculously recovered from its ashes, and you have a picture of my uncle the professor!

But marvel reached its climax when, running across the volcanic dust, he seized a bare skull, and cried in vibrating tones.

'Axel! Axel! a human head!'

'A human head, Uncle?' I replied, not less confounded.

'Yes, my boy. Oh, Mr. Milne-Edwards! Oh, M. de Quatrefages, why aren't you here with me!'

THIRTY-EIGHT

MY UNCLE LECTURES

To explain the significance of this invocation of some distinguished scientists, it must be recalled that an event of great importance in palæontology had taken place some time before our departure.

On the 28th of March, 1863, some workmen under the direction of M. Boucher, of Perthes, had unearthed a human jaw-bone from fourteen feet below the soil, in a quarry near Abbeville in France. It was the first fossil of this kind brought up to the light of day. Near it there were stone hatchets and chipped flints.

This discovery made a great noise, not only in France, but also in Britain and Germany. Many geologists, including in France the names of Milne-Edwards and de Quatrefages, and in Germany, amongst others, that of Lidenbrock, were enthusiastic believers in the new discovery.

They were, however, vigorously opposed by M. Elie de Beaumont, who held that the strata in which the jaw had been found were less ancient than had been supposed, and that man did not co-exist with the animals of the Quaternary epoch. M. de Beaumont was, however, practically alone in his opinion, and as a matter of fact, since our departure, though of course we did not know it at the time, further discoveries of human remains had strengthened the belief in the antiquity of man.

The astonishment, then, and joy of my uncle will become comprehensible, especially when, twenty paces farther on, he found himself face to face with a complete specimen of Quaternary man.

It was a human body, perfectly preserved, whether by some peculiarity of the soil, like that of the cemetery of Saint Michael at Bordeaux, or by some other agency, I do not know. At any rate this body, with stretched, parchment-like skin, limbs still covered with muscle—apparently at any rate—perfect teeth, a mass of hair, long nails on fingers and toes, was presented to our eyes as in life.

I was mute in the presence of this dweller in another age. My uncle, usually so ready with words, was silent too. We raised the body against a rock. He looked at us from his hollow eye-sockets. We beat on his sonorous chest.

Then my uncle became once more the professor, and forgetting the meagre attendance at his lecture, he launched forth into a discourse on the age-old corpse, proving satisfactorily that it was of the Caucasian type, in spite of its antiquity, that the man had been less than six feet high, contrary to what some people would expect, and that he was undoubtedly contemporaneous with the Mastodon and other monsters whose bones surrounded us. When he ceased speaking, his audience broke out into unanimous applause!

This indeed was not the only human body we came across—there were others, along with the animals. But we were not at present prepared to solve the question whether these remains had slipped down at the time of some convulsion of the earth, or whether the living beings had passed their existence in this extraordinary region.

THIRTY-NINE

WAS IT A MAN?

For another half-hour we walked over these bones, led on by eager curiosity. What other wonders did this cavern hold, what scientific treasures?

The sea-shore had long since disappeared behind the bone-covered hills. The imprudent professor, heedless of the risk of losing our way, led me on and on. We advanced in silence, bathed in the waves of electric light. And I am still unable to explain the fact that this light was so equally diffused that it shone uniformly on all sides of objects. It did not come from a definite spot, and consequently there were no shadows. All vapour had disappeared; it seemed like mid-day in the equatorial regions, and we resembled the fantastic personage in Hoffmann's tale, who had lost his shadow.

After walking about a mile, we saw the edge of an immense forest, but not a forest of mushrooms, like that near Port Gräuben.

This showed the vegetation of the Tertiary Period in all its splendour. Great palms, of species now unknown, pines, yews, cypress, and thujas were there, joined together by a network of impenetrable lianas. The ground was carpeted with moss and hepaticas. Streams murmured under their shade, if shade it could be called, and on the banks of these

Enormous forms were moving beneath the trees

grew tree-ferns, such as are grown in our hot-houses. Colour, however, was wanting to these trees, shrubs, and plants, deprived of the vivifying rays of the sun. They were all of one uniform hue, brownish and faded-looking. The leaves had no green, and the very flowers, so numerous in the Tertiary age which saw their first appearance, were without colour or perfume, and seemed made of bleached paper.

My uncle ventured into this gigantic thicket, and I followed, but not without a certain apprehension. Where nature had provided such vast stores of vegetable food, might there not be great mammals to be met with?

Suddenly I stopped, holding my uncle back. The diffused light made it possible to distinguish objects in the depths of the wood. I thought I saw—no, I *did* see enormous forms moving beneath the trees! It was indeed a herd of Mastodons, no longer fossil, but *living*, and resembling those whose remains were discovered in 1801 in the marshes of Ohio! I saw these great elephants with trunks curling about below the trees like a legion of serpents. I heard the sound of their great tusks as they tore at the bark of the ancient trees. The branches cracked, and the leaves torn off in masses disappeared into the great throats of the monsters.

My uncle was gazing. Suddenly he seized me by the arm crying: 'Come on! Forward! Forward!'

'No,' I answered, 'no! We have no weapons! What could we do against these giant quadrupeds? No human creature could brave their anger with impunity!'

'No human creature?' said my uncle, lowering his voice. 'You are wrong, Axel! Look, look, over there! It seems to me that I see a living being—a being like us—a *man*!'

I looked, shrugging my shoulders, and determined not to yield to credulity. But struggle to disbelieve as I might, the

G
193

evidence was too strong. There, less than a quarter of a mile away, leaning against the trunk of an enormous kauri tree, was a human being, keeping the great flock of Mastodons!

Immanis pecoris custos, immanior ipse. Yes! *immanior ipse*! This was not like the fossil creature whose body we had found among the bones; he was a giant capable of commanding these monsters. He was more than twelve feet high. His head, as big as that of a buffalo, was half hidden in his wild locks—a veritable mane, like that of the primitive elephants. He was brandishing in his hand an enormous bough—a worthy crook for this antediluvian shepherd!

We remained motionless, stupefied. But we might be perceived, and must fly at once.

'Come, come!' I cried, dragging my uncle, who for the first time gave in to me.

A quarter of an hour later, we were out of sight of this redoubtable enemy. And now when I can think quietly, months after these events—*was* it a man? No, impossible! No human creature *could* be living in that underground world. I would rather believe it was some extraordinary monkey—though none of the prehistoric monkeys approached that size! Never mind, however unlikely, it *was* a monkey, a monkey, I tell you, and not a man! Never a man!

We wandered in stupefaction, instinctively making our way to the Lidenbrock Sea, and I kept thinking that we must be near Port Gräuben, for the shape of the rocks, and the streams and cascades reminded me of it.

'Evidently,' I said to my uncle, 'we have not come back exactly to our point of departure, but if we skirt the coast, no doubt we shall reach Port Gräuben.'

'In that case,' said my uncle, 'it will be best to return to the raft. But are you not mistaken, Axel?'

'It is difficult to be sure, the rocks are all so much alike. But it seems to me that is the promontory at the foot of which Hans built the raft.'

'Well, but then, Axel, we should see some traces of ourselves, and I see nothing——'

'But *I* do!' I cried, springing towards an object which was shining on the sand.

'What is it, then?'

'There!' I answered, showing my uncle a dagger I had just picked up!

'Really!' he said, 'you brought this with you?'

'No, *I* didn't, but you did, I suppose?'

'Not to my knowledge; I have never possessed such a thing.'

'Still less I, Uncle.'

'That's peculiar.'

'No, it's quite simple; Icelanders often have weapons of this kind, and Hans must be the owner of this, and have dropped it on the beach.'

'Hans!' said my uncle, shaking his head.

Then he examined the weapon attentively, and said gravely:

'Axel, this dagger dates from the sixteenth century, and is of Spanish origin. It belongs neither to you nor to me, nor yet to our guide.'

'Do you mean to say——'

'Look, the blade is coated with rust, nor of a day nor of a year, but of centuries!'

The professor, as usual, became animated, as his imagination ran away with him.

'Axel,' he resumed; 'we are on the eve of the great discovery! This blade has remained on the sand one, two, three hundred years, and has been notched by use on the rocks of this subterranean sea!'

'But it could not have come alone!' I cried. 'Someone must have preceded us!'

'Yes, a man.'

'And that man——?'

'That man has engraved his name with this dagger. He wished once more to indicate the path to the centre. Come, let us search!'

With intense interest we now examined the high cliffs, seeking for the smallest clefts which might lead to a gallery.

Presently we came to a place where the shore narrowed; the sea came up nearly to the feet of the rock-buttresses, leaving only about six feet between. Between two projecting rocks there appeared the entrance to a dark tunnel.

There, on a slab of granite, appeared two mysterious letters, half worn away—the two initials of the bold, fantastic traveller

'A. S.,' cried my uncle. 'Arne Saknussemm! Arne Saknussemm once more!'

FORTY

AN OBSTACLE

Since our journey began, I had been astonished many times; I should have thought myself immune from surprise and incapable of wonder. But at the sight of those two letters, cut there three centuries before, I fell into an amazement bordering on utter stupidity. Not only was the signature of the learned alchemist legible on the rock, but I also held in my hand the pen which had traced it. Unless I were outrageously sceptical, I could no longer doubt the existence of the traveller and the reality of his expedition.

While these thoughts whirled in my brain, Professor Lidenbrock was indulging in a panegyric on Arne Saknussemm.

'Marvellous genius!' he cried. 'You have neglected nothing which could open up to other mortals the passages through the crust of the earth, and your fellows can find the traces of your footsteps, three centuries old! Your name, engraved at intervals, leads on the traveller bold enough to follow you, and at the very centre of our planet it will be found again, inscribed by your own hand! Well, I too will sign my name on this page of granite. But at any rate, let this cape seen by you in this sea discovered by you be known for ever as Cape Saknussemm!'

This, or something like it, was what I heard, and I too felt my enthusiasm catching fire from his; I forgot the dangers of the journey and the perils of the return. What another had done I would do too. 'Forward, forward!' I cried.

I was already springing towards the dark gallery, when the professor stopped me; he, the impulsive one, counselled patience and calm, saying: 'Let us first return to Hans, and bring the raft to this place.'

I obeyed, not without reluctance, and slipped away rapidly among the rocks on the shore.

'Do you know, Uncle,' said I, as we walked, 'we have been singularly favoured by circumstances so far!'

'Oh, you think so, Axel?'

'Yes, for even the storm itself served to put us in the right way. Thank God for it! It brought us back to this side, which we should have left behind in fine weather. If our prow (the prow of a *raft*!) had touched the southern shores of the Lidenbrock Sea, what would have become of us? We should never have seen the name of Saknussemm, and should now have been desolately wandering on a shore with no outlet!'

'Yes, Axel, there is something providential in the fact that, sailing southwards, we should have turned and come northwards to Cape Saknussemm. But it seems to me *more* than astonishing—I can't explain it at all.'

'Well, *that* doesn't matter. It's more important to take advantage of facts than to explain them.'

'No doubt, my boy, but——'

'But now we shall go north again, under Sweden, Russia, Siberia, I dare say! That's better than the deserts of Africa or the waves of the ocean!'

'Yes, and anything is better than this horizontal sea, which takes us nowhere. Now we shall go down, and down, and down! Do you know that we're not much more than 4000 miles from the centre now?'

'And what's that?' I cried. 'Not worth talking about!'

This insane conversation continued when we had rejoined the guide. Everything was ready for the start—not a package out of place. We boarded the raft, the sail was hoisted, and Hans steered, following the coast, for Cape Saknussemm.

The wind was not very favourable, and the rocks often obliged us to make long detours, but with the help of our iron-shod staves we managed in three hours, that is by about 6 p.m., to reach a spot where we could disembark.

I sprang ashore, still eager, and proposing even to 'burn our boats' so as to cut off all possibility of retreat. But my uncle demurred, and struck me as rather lukewarm.

'At least,' I said, 'let us start without losing an instant.'

'Yes, my boy, but first let us examine this new gallery, to see if our ladders will be wanted.'

My uncle put his Ruhmkorff apparatus into working order. The raft, moored to the bank, was left to itself; anyway, the opening of the gallery was only about twenty yards away, and our little party, with myself for leader, at once made for it.

The almost circular opening had a diameter of about five feet; the dark tunnel was scooped out of the living rock, and smoothly bored by the eruptive materials which had formerly passed through it; the lower part just touched the ground, so that it was easy to get into it.

We followed an almost horizontal course, when, about six paces along, our steps were obstructed by an enormous block.

'Confound the rock!' I cried in anger, seeing myself stopped by an insurmountable obstacle.

In vain we searched to right and left, beneath and above;

there was no passage. I was bitterly disappointed, and inclined to deny the reality of the obstacle.

'What about Saknussemm?' I cried.

'Yes,' said my uncle, 'was *he* stopped by this stone door?'

'No, no,' I exclaimed, 'it must have come there since, as a result of volcanic activity; and if we can't remove it, we are unworthy to reach the centre of the earth!'

'Well,' said my uncle, 'with our pickaxes——'

'It's too hard for pickaxes.'

'But——'

'*I* know! Let's blow it up! All we've got to do is to break up a bit of rock!'

'Hans, come on, set to work!' cried my uncle.

The Icelander went to the raft, and soon returned with a pickaxe with which he made a hollow for the explosive. It was no slight task—he had to make a hole big enough to hold fifty pounds of gun-cotton, the explosive force of which is four times as great as that of gunpowder.

I was in an extreme of excitement. While Hans was working, I eagerly helped my uncle to prepare a long match made of damp gunpowder in a tube formed from linen.

'We shall get through,' said I.

'We shall get through,' repeated my uncle.

At midnight, our mine was complete; the charge of gun-cotton was packed in the hollow of the rock, and the match, passing along the gallery, came to an end just outside. A spark would now suffice to set free the terrific latent force.

'Tomorrow,' said the professor.

I was obliged to resign myself to waiting six long hours more!

FORTY-ONE

DOWNWARDS!

Next day, Thursday, 27th August, was a great date in the subterranean journey. I cannot even now think of it without feeling my heart beat with fear. From that time on, our reason, our judgment, our ingenuity, went for nothing, and we became merely the playthings of the forces of the earth.

At six we were up. The moment had arrived to force our way through the granite crust. I begged for the honour of firing the mine. Having done so, I was to join my companions on the raft, still loaded with our effects; then we should sail away from the shore, to avoid the dangers of the explosion, which might not confine itself to the interior of the rock.

We calculated that the match would burn for ten minutes before the spark reached the gun-cotton, so I had time enough to reach the raft. I prepared to carry out my task, not without a certain emotion.

After a hasty meal, my uncle and the guide embarked, while I remained on the shore.

'Go, my boy,' said my uncle, 'and then come back to us at once.'

'You may be sure I won't stop to play, Uncle.'

I went to the opening of the gallery, opened my lantern, and took hold of the end of the match.

The professor stood with the chronometer in his hand. 'Are you ready?' he cried.

'Yes, I'm ready.'

'Well then, fire, my boy!'

I quickly plunged the match into the flame, saw it begin to crackle, and ran back to the shore.

'Get on,' said my uncle, 'and we'll push off.'

Hans, with a vigorous push, started us away, and we found ourselves perhaps fifty feet from the beach.

It was a thrilling time. The professor watched the hand of the chronometer.

'Five minutes more,' he said. 'Four, three.'

My pulse was beating half-seconds.

'Two. One. Now, granite mountains, make way!'

What *did* happen then? I don't think I heard the noise of the explosion. But the form of the rocks suddenly changed before my eyes; they opened like a curtain. I saw a fathomless abyss dug through the shore. The sea, seized with a fit of dizziness, became one immense wave, on the back of which the raft stood up perpendicularly.

We were all thrown over. In less than a second, the light was replaced by profound darkness. Then I felt that there was no longer any support, not for my feet, but for the raft. I tried to speak to my uncle, but the roar of the water made it impossible.

However, in spite of the darkness, the noise, surprise, and emotion, I realized what had happened.

Beyond the rock we had blown up, there was an abyss. The explosion had brought about a sort of earthquake in the much-fissured rock, a way to the abyss had opened, and the sea, pouring down like a torrent, was carrying us along with it. I felt we were lost!

An hour, perhaps two, passed thus. We linked our arms and held each other's hands, so as not to be thrown off the raft; we were violently shaken whenever it struck the wall. However, this happened seldom, whence I concluded that the passage was growing wider.

It was obviously the path followed by Saknussemm; but instead of going alone, we had by our imprudence brought the sea down along with us!

These ideas, of course, presented themselves to my mind in a vague and obscure form. I brought them together with difficulty during the wild descent which seemed almost like a fall. Judging by the rush of air whipping my face, we were going faster than an express train. To light a torch was therefore impossible, and our last electric apparatus had been broken by the explosion.

I was therefore much surprised when I suddenly saw a light close to me, illuminating the calm countenance of Hans. The skilful guide had succeeded in lighting the lantern, and though its flame shook so that it nearly went out, still it shed some little light amid the awful darkness.

The tunnel was certainly broad. Our feeble light did not show us both sides at once. The slope down which the water was careering was greater than that of the most celebrated rapids in America; the surface seemed like a sheaf of liquid arrows in vigorous flight. Sometimes there were eddies which made the raft spin round; when it went near the walls I threw the light of the lamp on them, and got some idea of our speed by the way in which projections of rock were prolonged into lines, so that we seemed to be encircled by a network of such lines. I estimated that we might be travelling at a rate of ninety miles an hour.

Hours went by. In attempting to arrange our belongings,

I discovered that most of them had disappeared at the time of the explosion, when the sea assailed us so violently. Of our instruments, only the compass and the chronometer remained. The ladders and ropes were represented by one bit of cord rolled round the remains of the mast. Not a pick-axe left, and worst of all, not a day's food! The most careful search failed to discover more than one piece of dried meat and a few biscuits.

Were we to die of hunger? Strange to say, in the thought of this future peril I forgot the present imminent risk. However, I had sufficient self-control to spare my uncle the knowledge of my discovery.

At this moment the light of the lantern flickered and then went out. The wick had burned to its end, and we were in utter darkness, which we could not attempt to dissipate. There was a torch left, but it could not be lighted; so, like a child, I closed my eyes against the darkness.

After a considerable lapse of time, our speed was re-doubled, as I perceived by the wind on my face. It now seemed like an almost vertical fall. My uncle and Hans both held me firmly by the arms. Suddenly, after a very short time, I felt a shock; the raft had not encountered a hard substance, but its fall was arrested. A great column of liquid seemed to rise and flood its surface, so that I found myself drowning—unable to breathe.

This sudden inundation, however, did not last. In a few seconds my lungs were breathing fresh air. My uncle and Hans were gripping my arms so that they were bruised, and the raft was still carrying all three.

FORTY-TWO

OUR LAST MEAL

I suppose it was then about ten o'clock at night. The first of my senses to function after this last experience was the sense of hearing. I noticed that silence had taken the place of the roaring of the water which had so long filled my ears. Then I heard my uncle say:

'We are rising.'

'What *do* you mean?' I cried.

'Yes, rising, rising.'

I put out my hand and touched the wall; I drew it back bleeding. We were rising with extreme rapidity.

'The torch! The torch!' cried the professor, and Hans, with difficulty, managed to light it. The flame was blown downward, but still gave light enough to show us that we were in a narrow shaft, twenty feet or so across.

'The water has reached as low as it can go,' said my uncle, 'and is rising now to find its own level, carrying us with it.'

'But if there is no outlet, we shall be crushed!'

'Axel,' said the professor very calmly, 'the situation is almost desperate, but as there are some slight chances of escape, I propose that we should renew our strength by eating.'

'Eating?' I repeated.

'Yes, without delay,' and he spoke in Danish to Hans, who shook his head.

'What?' cried my uncle, 'all our provisions gone?'

'Yes, this is all that is left—one piece of dried meat for the three of us!'

We looked at each other; an hour passed, and I began to suffer terribly from hunger. So did the others, but none of us would touch the poor remains of our food. We were still rising with a rapidity which sometimes took our breath away, as it does with aeronauts when they ascend too fast. But instead of suffering from cold, as they do, we began to experience a continual rise of temperature—it was now quite 40° C., and I said to the professor:

'If we are neither drowned nor crushed, and do not die of hunger, we have still the chance of being burned alive.'

He only shrugged his shoulders and plunged into thought again. An hour later he broke the silence by saying:

'Well, we had better make up our minds to it.'

'Make up our minds to what?'

'To eating the rest of our food, and keeping up our strength, so that if a chance of rescue presents itself, we may be vigorous enough to take it.'

'But don't you *yet* despair?'

'No!'

'What! You believe there's a chance of escape?'

'Yes, certainly; I don't think a being endowed with will-power should ever despair, as long as his heart beats.'

What words! The man who could utter them in such circumstances was certainly of no common mould.

'Well, let us eat, then!' I said.

My uncle took the piece of meat and the biscuits, and divided them scrupulously into three equal parts; it made about a pound of food apiece. Hans had discovered a flask full of gin, and this revived me a little.

'Forträffig!' said Hans, drinking in his turn.

'Excellent!' repeated my uncle.

A little hope had returned to me, though we had eaten our last meal. It was then five o'clock in the morning. After this, each followed his own thoughts. What were those of Hans, the extreme Westerner, with the Oriental type of fatalistic resignation? As for me, my thoughts were but memories—memories of the house in the Königstrasse, of my dear Gräuben and the good Martha, and the deep growlings which shook the earth seemed to me the sounds of traffic in a great city.

My uncle on his part, torch in hand, was examining the nature of the rock with a view to estimating our possible position; I heard him using geological expressions which I understood, and I began to be interested in spite of myself.

'Eruptive granite,' he said; 'still at the primitive epoch, but we are rising—who knows?' Later he added:

'Gneiss now! Mica-schist! Good! We are in the Transition Period, and then——'

Meanwhile the temperature was rising so that I was bathed in perspiration. We were all three obliged to take off our coats and waistcoats; any clothes at all became a source of discomfort, if not of pain.

'Are we rising up to an incandescent furnace?' I cried, as the heat redoubled.

'No,' replied my uncle, 'It's impossible!'

'And yet,' I said, touching the wall, 'this wall is burning hot.'

Immediately after, my hand having touched the water, I withdrew it in all haste.

'The water is boiling!' I cried.

This time the professor only replied by an angry gesticulation.

Then an invincible terror took possession of me, and I could not get rid of it. An idea, at first vague and undecided, became a certainty to my mind; I tried to repel it, but it obstinately returned. Some casual observations confirmed the idea; by the poor light of the torch, I noticed strange movements in the beds of rock. I resolved to observe the compass.

It had gone mad!

FORTY-THREE

AN ERUPTION!

Yes, mad! The needle was swinging round from one direction to the opposite in sharp jerks, indicating every point of the compass in turn, as if it had been seized with giddiness.

I knew that, according to received theories, the crust of the earth is never in a state of complete rest; the effects of chemical decomposition, currents of water, magnetic forces, and so on tend to produce constant movements, even though the beings living on the surface may be unaware of them. This phenomenon alone, therefore, would not have given rise in my mind to the dread suspicion that filled it.

But other facts of a special kind could no longer be ignored; detonations multiplied with an alarming intensity; I could only compare them with the noise of a great number of vehicles rapidly driven across a pavement.

It was a continuous thunder.

Then, the mad compass, affected by the electric phenomena, confirmed me in my opinion; the fissure would be filled up, and we, poor atoms, should be crushed in the terrible meeting of the walls!

'Uncle! Uncle,' I cried, 'we are lost!'

'What is this new alarm?' he answered with surprising calm. 'What's the matter?'

'What's the matter? Look at the walls moving, the torrid heat, the boiling water, the clouds of vapour, the antics of the needle—all these signs of an earthquake!'

My uncle gently shook his head.

'My boy, I think you are mistaken.'

'What? Do you not recognize these symptoms?'

'Not of an *earthquake*. Better than that, I think!'

'What do you mean?'

'An eruption, Axel.'

'An eruption! Are we in the vent of an active volcano?'

"I think so,' said the professor, smiling. 'And it's the best thing that could happen to us.'

Was my uncle mad? What did his words mean? How could he be calm and smiling?

'What!' I cried, 'we are in the midst of an eruption! Fate has thrown us into the path of incandescent lava, of molten rock, and boiling water! We are to be flung hither and thither, expelled, rejected, belched forth into the air along with masses of rock, and rains of ashes and scoriæ, in a burst of flame! And that's the best thing that could happen to us!'

'Yes,' said the professor, looking at me over the top of his spectacles, 'for it's the only chance we have of returning to the surface of the earth!'

I pass rapidly over the thousand ideas which then crossed each other in my brain. My uncle was right, perfectly right, and never had he appeared more audacious nor more convinced than at the moment in which he was calmly expecting and calculating on the chances of an eruption.

Still we rose, our ascent continuing throughout the night. The noise became ever louder, I was almost suffocated, I thought my last hour was at hand, and yet imagination is so capricious that I gave myself up to a really childish speculation. But I was at the mercy of my thoughts—I had no control over them!

It was evident that we were being thrown up by an eruptive impulse; under the raft there was boiling water, and under

that a mass of lava, containing rocks which when thrown out of the crater, would be dispersed in every direction. There was no doubt then that we were in the vent of a volcano.

But this time, instead of the extinct volcano Snaefells, it was one in vigorous activity. So I was wondering what mountain it could be, and in what part of the world we were to be flung out.

In some northern region, of course. Before its late vagaries, the compass had consistently pointed to that. Since leaving Cape Saknussemm, we had been carried due north for many hundreds of miles. Now, had we come back under Iceland? Were we to issue from the crater of Hecla or of one of the seven other volcanoes of the island? In that latitude, to the west I could only think of the little-known volcanoes of the north-west coast of America. In the east, there was only one, Esk, in Jan Mayen's Land, not far from Spitzbergen. I could not help speculating as to which of these was ours.

Towards morning our ascent became yet more rapid, and there could no longer be any doubt as to the cause of it. Soon lurid reflections appeared on the walls of the chimney, which was seen to be widening; on either hand I saw deep cuttings, like immense tunnels, sending forth thick smoke, while tongues of flame crackled and licked the walls.

'Look, look, Uncle!' I cried.

'Well, those are sulphur flames. Nothing more natural in an eruption.'

'But if they close round us?'

'They won't close round us.'

'But if we are suffocated?'

'We shan't be suffocated; the shaft is getting wider, and if necessary we'll leave the raft and take shelter in some crack.'

'But the water! The rising water!'

'There's no water left, Axel, but a sort of viscous lava-stream which is carrying us up with it to the mouth of the crater.'

It was true that the water had disappeared, giving place to heavy, though boiling, rocky material. The temperature became unbearably high; a thermometer would have marked over 70° C.! I was bathed in perspiration, and but for the rapidity of the ascent, we should certainly have been suffocated.

However, the professor did not follow out his own idea of leaving the raft, and it was as well. Those few planks, roughly joined together, gave us a footing which we should have sought in vain elsewhere.

Towards 8 a.m. there was at last a change. The ascent suddenly stopped, and the raft became absolutely motionless.

'What is it?' I asked, shaken by this unexpected stoppage.

'A halt,' answered my uncle.

'Is the eruption at an end?'

'I'm sure I hope not.'

I stood up and tried to look round. Perhaps the raft had caught against a rock for a moment. If so, it ought to be freed at once. But it was not so. The columns of ashes, scoriæ, and molten rock had itself ceased to rise.

'Ah!' said my uncle with set teeth, 'never fear, my boy, this calm is only temporary; it has lasted five minutes, and soon we shall be off again.'

He kept his eye on his chronometer, and soon he was proved to be right. The raft was set in motion again, and rose in a rapid and disorderly manner for about two minutes —then it stopped again.

'Good,' said my uncle, noting the time. 'In ten minutes it is due to start.'

'Ten minutes?'

'Yes; this is an intermittent volcano, and it lets us take our breath when *it* does.'

Nothing could be more exact. At the given minute we were shot upward again with extreme velocity; we had to cling to the planks to keep from being thrown out. Then the pressure ceased.

213

How many times this happened, I cannot say; all I can affirm is that at each fresh ascent we were impelled with an increasing force, and as it were converted into an actual projectile. During the pauses one was nearly suffocated; during the motion, the burning air took my breath away. I thought of the bliss of suddenly finding myself in the Polar regions, at a temperature of 30° below zero! My excited imagination pictured the snowy plains of the Arctic regions, and I longed to roll on the icy carpet of the Pole! But gradually my head, confused by the reiterated shocks, gave way. But for the arms of Hans, more than once my skull would have been dashed against the wall.

I have therefore no clear memory of what happened during the hours that followed, only a confused consciousness of perpetual detonations, of earth-movements, and of an eddying motion which was imparted to the raft. It rose and fell on waves of lava, in the midst of a rain of ashes, and surrounded by roaring flames. A wind which seemed to come from an immense bellows kept up the subterranean fire. One last time the face of Hans appeared to me in the light of the flames, and I understood the feelings of the criminal fastened to the mouth of the cannon, at the moment when the shot is fired which disperses his members into the air.

FORTY-FOUR

WHERE ARE WE?

When I re-opened my eyes, I felt the strong hand of the guide on my waist-belt. With the other hand he was holding my uncle. I was not seriously injured, only bruised and shaken all over. I found myself lying on the slope of a mountain, only a few paces from a precipice down which the least movement would have impelled me. Hans had saved me from death while I was rolling down the external slopes of the crater.

'Where are we?' asked my uncle, who appeared to be much annoyed at returning to the surface.

The guide shrugged his shoulders to express his ignorance.

'In Iceland?' said I.

'Nej,' replied Hans.

'What, not in Iceland?' cried the professor.

'Hans must be wrong,' I said, rising.

After the innumerable surprises of the expedition, one more had been reserved for us. I expected to see a cone covered with eternal snow, in the midst of arid Arctic deserts, under the pale rays of the polar heavens; but contrary to these expectations, we found ourselves halfway down a mountain baked by the heat of the sun, which was scorching us with its rays.

I was not prepared to trust my eyes; but the veritable roasting to which my body was subjected admitted of no doubt. We had come out of the crater half-naked, and the radiant luminary, from whom we had demanded nothing for two months, was lavishing on us floods of heat and light.

When my eyes had become accustomed to these rays, I used them to rectify the errors of my imagination. But I was determined to be at least in Spitzbergen—I could not make up my mind to give in so easily.

The professor spoke first, saying: 'It certainly doesn't look like Iceland.'

'But Jan Mayen's Land?' I suggested.

'No, it's not that either, my boy. This is not a northern volcano with its granite sides and its snow-cap.'

'And yet——'

'Look, Axel, look!'

Above our heads, not more than five hundred feet away, was the crater of the volcano, through which, every ten minutes, there was shot out, with a very loud explosion, a tall column of flame, mingled with pumice-stone, ashes and lava. I felt the mountain heave as it breathed like a whale, casting up fire and air at intervals through its enormous nostrils. Below us, on a fairly steep slope, layers of eruptive material were seen extending to a depth of seven or eight hundred feet. The base of the mountain was hidden in a regular garland of green trees, amongst which I distinguished olives, figs, and vines loaded with ripe grapes.

It certainly did not fit in with one's notions of the Arctic regions!

When one's gaze passed beyond this girdle of verdure, it wandered over the waters of an exquisite sea or lake, in the midst of which this enchanted land appeared to be an island not many miles in diameter. On the east appeared a little port, with a few houses round it, and sheltering in its harbour some boats of a peculiar kind, floating on the blue water. Beyond, groups of small islets rose from the liquid plain, so numerous as to resemble a great ant-heap. To the west, far-away shores showed rounded on the horizon; on some there were blue mountains of exquisite outline, on others, farther away, there was an immensely high cone, from the summit of which floated a banner of smoke. In the north, an immense stretch of water sparkled in the rays of the sun, showing here and there the top of a mast, or a sail swelling with the wind.

The unexpectedness of such a scene multiplied its wonderful beauty a hundred times.

'Where are we? Where *are* we?' I once more murmured.

Hans shut his eyes indifferently, and my uncle gazed without comprehension.

'Whatever this mountain may be,' he said at last, 'it's rather hot; the explosions are still going on, and it would be a pity to have come out of the volcano only to be knocked on the head by a rock. So let us come down, and find out where we are. Besides, I am dying of hunger and thirst.'

Certainly the professor was not a contemplative. For my part, forgetting all needs and fatigues, I could have stayed at that spot for hours longer, but I was obliged to follow my companions.

The stones thrown out by the volcano formed very steep slopes; we slipped into veritable quicksands of ashes, avoiding the lava-streams which wound like fiery serpents. As we descended, I began to talk volubly, for my imagination was so stimulated that it overflowed in words.

'We are in Asia,' I cried, 'on the coasts of India, in the

217

Malay Archipelago, or in Oceania! We have gone half across the earth, and come out at the Antipodes!'

'But the compass!' said my uncle.

'Oh, the compass!' I said with embarrassment.

'According to it, we were going steadily north.'

'Then did it lie?'

'Lie! No!'

'Then *is* this the North Pole?'

'No, not the Pole, but——'

The matter was inexplicable; I did not know what to think.

However, we were approaching the verdure which was so good to look upon. I was tormented by hunger and thirst. Fortunately, after walking for two hours, we came into a lovely countryside, completely covered with olives, pomegranates, and vines which seemed to be common property. Besides, in our state of destitution, we were not disposed to be over-scrupulous. What a joy it was to press these delicious fruits against our lips, and to bite whole clusters of the purple grapes! Not far off, in the grass under the welcome shade of the trees, I found a spring of fresh water, into which it was bliss to plunge our faces and hands.

While we were thus given over to all the joys of repose, a child appeared between two groups of olives.

'Ah!' I cried, 'there is an inhabitant of this fortunate land!'

He was a poor little miserably clothed, sickly creature, apparently much alarmed by our appearance; indeed, half-naked as we were, and with neglected hair and beards, we certainly must have had an ill-conditioned aspect, and unless it was a country of robbers, we were likely to be a source of alarm to the inhabitants.

Just as the urchin was about to take flight, Hans ran after him and brought him back, in spite of his cries and kicks.

218

My uncle began by soothing him as well as he could, and asked in German:

'What is the name of this mountain, little friend?'

The child made no answer.

'Good,' said my uncle, 'we are not in Germany.'

He then put the same question in English.

Still the child did not answer. I was much interested.

'Is he dumb?' cried the professor, who then (very proud of his linguistic powers) repeated his question in French.

The child was still silent.

'Then let's try Italian,' resumed my uncle, and said to him in that tongue:

'Dove siamo?'

'Yes, where are we?' I repeated impatiently. The little boy said nothing.

'Bother the child! *Will* you answer!' cried my uncle, who was getting angry and shaking the urchin by the ears. 'Come si chiama questa isola?'

'Stromboli,' answered the little peasant, escaping from the grasp of Hans and darting off to the plain, through the olives.

We were not thinking about *him*! Stromboli! What an effect did this unexpected name produce on my imagination! We were in the midst of the Mediterranean, surrounded by the scenes of ancient mythology, in that Strongyle where Æolus held winds and tempests on the chain. And those blue mountains on the east were the mountains of Calabria! And that volcano far away to the south was Etna, the great and terrible!

'Stromboli! Stromboli!' I repeated.

My uncle accompanied me with gestures and words; it was as if we were singing a chorus.

Oh, what a journey! What a wonderful journey! We had

gone in by one volcano and come out by another, and this other was 4000 miles away from Snaefells and the barren shores of Iceland on the far edge of the inhabited world! The chances of our expedition had carried us into the midst of the most fortunate countries of our globe! We had exchanged the regions of eternal snow for those of eternal verdure, and the grey fogs of the cold north for the azure skies of Sicily!

Refreshed by our delicious repast, we set out again to reach the port of Stromboli. It did not seem advisable to say how we had arrived in the island; the superstitious Italians would certainly have believed us to be demons thrown up from hell, so we resigned ourselves to passing simply as victims of shipwreck. It was less glorious but safer.

On the way I heard my uncle murmuring: 'But the compass—it *did* point to the north! What can be the explanation?'

'Really,' said I, with an air of disdain, 'it's much simpler to let it alone!'

'It would be a disgrace to a professor at the Johannæum if he could not discover the reason for a cosmic phenomenon!'

Thus speaking, my uncle, half-naked, with his leather purse-girdle round his waist and settling his spectacles on his nose, became once more the terrible professor of mineralogy.

An hour after leaving the olive-wood we arrived at the port of San Vincenzio, where Hans demanded his wages for his thirteenth week of service, which were counted out to him along with hearty handshakes.

At that moment, if he did not altogether share our very natural emotion, at least he gave vent to a most unusual display of sentiment—he touched our hands gently with the ends of his fingers, and smiled.

FORTY-FIVE

———————◁○▷———————

CONCLUSION

This is the end of a tale which many people, however accustomed to being astonished at nothing, will refuse to believe. But I am steeled in advance against human incredulity.

We were received by the Stromboli fishermen with the kindness always extended to those who have suffered shipwreck, and obtained clothing and food. After waiting forty-eight hours, we were conveyed on the 31st of August to Messina, where some hours of good rest completed our recovery from all our fatigues.

On Friday, 4th September, we embarked on the *Volturno*, one of the French Imperial packet-boats, and three days later landed at Marseilles, our minds preoccupied with one problem, that of our accursed compass. This inexplicable circumstance continued seriously to worry me. On the evening of 9th September we arrived at Hamburg.

The stupefaction of Martha and the joy of Gräuben I will not attempt to describe.

'Now you are a hero,' said my dear fiancée, 'you will never have to leave me, Axel.'

I looked at her. She wept and smiled.

I leave it to be imagined whether the return of Professor Lidenbrock made a sensation in Hamburg. Owing to the indiscretions of Martha, the fact of his departure for the centre of the earth had spread all over the world. People refused to believe it, and when he returned they still refused.

However, the presence of Hans, and some information coming from Iceland, somewhat modified public opinion.

Then my uncle became a great man, and I became the nephew of a great man, which is also something to be. Hamburg gave a feast in our honour. There was a public meeting at the Johannæum, at which the professor held forth on our expedition, omitting only the part about the compass. On the same day, he deposited the document of Saknussemm amongst the archives of the town, and expressed his deep regret that circumstances, stronger than his will, had not permitted him to follow the steps of the Dane to the very centre of the earth. He was modest in his glory, and his reputation gained by it. Of course there were some who envied him, and he was obliged to engage in controversy with scientists of many lands.

In the midst of this, my uncle had a real grief. Hans, in spite of his entreaties, left Hamburg; the man to whom we owed everything would not let us pay our debt. He was seized with home-sickness.

'Färval,' said he one day, and with this simple good-bye, he left for Reykjawik, which he reached in safety. We were singularly attached to him; I shall never forget him, and I mean to see him again before I die.

In conclusion, I should say that the *Journey to the Centre of the Earth* made a tremendous sensation in the world. It was printed, and translated into all languages; it was commented on, discussed, attacked and defended with equal conviction on the part of the believers and the sceptics. As rarely happens, my uncle enjoyed during his lifetime all the fame he had merited, and indeed Mr. Barnum made him the the offer of 'exhibiting' him, at a very high remuneration, in the United States.

But a worry, which might almost be called a torment, mingled itself with this glory. This was the inexplicable behaviour of the compass. Now, for a scientist like my uncle, an unexplained fact is a torture to the mind. Well, Heaven had happiness in store for my uncle, after all.

One day, while arranging a collection of minerals in his study, I noticed the celebrated compass, and began to examine it. It had stayed there for six months, in its corner, without suspecting the fuss it was causing.

Suddenly I uttered a cry of surprise. The professor ran up to me.

'What is it?' he asked.

'The compass——'

'Well?'

'Well, the needle shows south where north is!'

'What are you saying?'

'Look! The poles are interchanged!'

My uncle looked, compared with another, and made the house shake by a wild leap.

What a light shone in on his mind and on mine!

'So,' he cried, when he had regained his powers of speech, 'after we arrived at Cape Saknussemm, the needle of this confounded compass showed south for north?'

'Evidently.'

'Then our error is explained. But what could possibly have caused this reversal of the poles?'

'It's very simple.'

'Explain yourself, my boy.'

'During the storm on the Lidenbrock Sea, that fire-ball,

which magnetized the iron on the raft, must have played this trick on our compass!'

'Ah!' cried the professor, bursting out laughing, 'it was a practical joke on the part of electricity!'

From that day onward, my uncle was the happiest of scientists, and I the happiest of men, for the pretty Gräuben entered the house at the Königstrasse in the double capacity of niece and wife. It is needless to add that her uncle was the illustrious Professor Otto Lidenbrock, a corresponding member of all the scientific, geographical, and mineralogical Societies of the five Continents.